MOVING ZEN

By C. W. Nicol

MOVING ZEN
FROM THE ROOF OF AFRICA

MOVING ZEN

Karate As a Way to Gentleness

C. W. Nicol

Drawings by Munehiro Ikeda

QUILL

New York 1982

Library of Congress Cataloging in Publication Data

Nicol, C. W. (Clive W.), 1940-
  Moving Zen.

  Originally published: New York : Morrow,
1975.
  1. Nicol, C. W. (Clive W.), 1940-
2. Martial artists—Great Britain—Biography.
3. Karate.   I. Title.
[GV1113.N5A33 1982]   796.8'153'0924   [B]   82-522
ISBN 0-688-02871-3   AACR2
ISBN 0-688-01181-0 (pbk.)

    3 4 5 6 7 8 9 10

BOOK DESIGN: HELEN ROBERTS

To Kanazawa Hirokazu

MOVING ZEN

∾ chapter one ∾

The Japanese character 先 "sen" means "ahead" or "before." The character 生 "sei" has the essence of many meanings—"life," "birth," "pure," "genuine," "raw." If the two characters are put together, they form the word "sensei," which is poorly translated as "teacher," and yet is the title given to teachers and to those people who demand great respect.

Mr. Takagi, or rather, Takagi sensei, was the director of the Japan Karate Association, which, in the early sixties, was the largest Karate organization in Japan. It was recognized by the Ministry of Education; its goal to improve and create wider interest in Karate. At first glance, Takagi sensei was not an imposing figure. He was shortish, round-faced, with the air of an affable, good-natured businessman. Yet his eyes carried the steel of the Karateka, the practitioner of Karate, and he held the fifth degree, or "dan" grade of black belt.

This was Tokyo, and I had come here, in the late fall of 1962 to devote myself to the study of martial arts, and in particular to the study of Karate, one of the deadliest systems of unarmed fighting in the world. But there are many paths to take, many styles to follow, and Takagi sensei had said at our first meeting, "There are other schools. Go to them and see, and then come back if you have truly decided to enter our school."

And so I went from place to place in Tokyo, visiting the dojo, or practice hall, of each of the main schools or styles of Karate. In Japan, Karate is followed as a religion is followed. The student can follow only one way, he cannot switch and change, or be fickle with his loyalties. It is not the Karate way.

I saw the Wado style. Its practitioners had movements that were graceful and flowing, and there I saw Karateka pitted against swordsman in a ritual ballet, and marveled at the lines of the body curving and leaping in and out of the range of the slicing steel, like a mongoose feinting at a cobra.

I saw the Goju style. It was powerful and menacing, and its followers developed iron-hard bodies through their special breathing exercises, and by dynamic tension and relaxation, moving in the dojo like angered tigers crouching in the bamboo, breath hissing and rasping through nostrils and throats, now moving slowly, slowly, and then with incredible swiftness. The school was dominated by the Master Yamaguchi, whom they call "The Cat." He wore his hair down to his shoulders, and was never seen in Western dress, preferring the somber dignity of kimono and the wide, skirt-like hakama, traditional male dress of Japan.

I went also to the dojo of the Shito school, and there saw a Karate that was straight and fast, with movements that were long and deep in the stances, closer to the Karate of the Japan Karate Association.

Lastly I visited the school of the Kyokushinkai. Approaching from Ikebukuro station (Ikebukuro is a part of Tokyo), I could hear the muffled chorus of yells. Vital and savage, the style was dominated by the presence and personality of the Master Oyama, perhaps the most famous and flamboyant Karateka now living, a man who had fought and killed bulls with his bare hands, who trained alone in the mountains and then descended to win the championships, who toured the United States, challenging all-comers, awing crowds with his displays of rock, brick and board breaking.

And then I returned to the headquarters of the Japan Karate Association, to the dojo of the style which outsiders call Shotokan. I liked it best.

Karate was brought to Japan from the southern islands of Okinawa in 1922. In introducing it, the Master Gichin Funakoshi, then ranking fifth dan black belt, had to impress the stern, somewhat chauvinistic warriors of mainland Japan. Frightening stories are told of the master's fights and exploits. Funakoshi sensei was a warrior, a poet and an artist, and his Karate indeed impressed an elite group who began to study under him. Some of these students became masters of their own accord, and became independent, setting up new styles and schools.

The Japan Karate Association was formed after World War Two, and until his death in 1957, Funakoshi sensei was the Chief Instructor. At the JKA the Karateka do not give their Karate any other name. They say it is simply Karate. However, other schools have called us Shotokan. "Shoto" was Funakoshi sensei's pen name; he was a great calligrapher, or artist of brush writing. "Kan" means building. So that "Shotokan-ryu" meant "the style they practice at Shoto's building."

The prototype of Karate was a secret fighting art developed in Okinawa. The people of that island group had been conquered and forbidden to carry arms. To defend themselves they developed an art which could, in the hands of a master, defeat an armed, armored man. Not only did they use feet and fists, but also mundane articles like the handle of a rice grinder, sickles, chains, sticks and small weapons easily disguised or hidden from their samurai overlords. It seems that the art as it was known in Okinawa was brought there from China. It was then an ancient art, with the lines of its ancestry vague and full of legends, connected to Shaolin temples, to Buddhist teachers, to warrior princes.

But it is the Japanese who have most assiduously developed it into a form that can be practiced as a sport, as well as a fighting art. They are a disciplined, idealistic people, and Karate as it is generally practiced in Japan is disciplined and idealistic.

Masters and pupils of each style tend to claim that their Karate is the best, the true Karate, and each will boast of the times that they have defeated other schools. Rivalry is fierce. However, I had seen the main styles, and been impressed, even awed, by all of them. I ignored the stories and chose the JKA because I liked it best, liked the good feeling I got from the headquarters dojo in Yotsuya. (Yotsuya is on Tokyo's Chuo line, and the dojo a few minutes' walk from the station.)

The Karate there was fast, powerful, with an emphasis on good form. The stances were low and deep, and punches and thrusts were generally straight and long. Movements were very precise and discipline extremely rigid. They were military in their training ways, yet not militant. It was stern, but friendly. Funakoshi sensei had been dead for five years, and if his photograph, his writings and his spirit presided over the dojo, they did so with a benevolent gentleness, not with a dominance that might have overpowered me, a Westerner. There was no one great teacher to be revered as a deity. There were many teachers, about thirty in all, and all of them were superb.

The Chief Instructor now was a quiet assuring gentleman. He too was a poet and a calligrapher. Masatoshi Nakayama, then ranking fifth dan,* began studying under Funakoshi sensei in 1931. In 1937 he went to Peking to study the Chinese language and various styles of Chinese fighting. Besides being Chief Instructor of the JKA, he is also director of physical education at the toughest martial-arts-conscious university in Japan—Takushoku University. All of the instructors were university graduates, and most, if not all of them, held black belt ranks in other fighting arts, such as Judo and Kendo (Japanese fencing). It was with confidence that I decided to place my body and my mind under the training of these men, and thus was to begin a two-and-a-half-year apprenticeship as a full-time student of Karate.

The Yotsuya dojo was housed in an old, rickety building, and the front door was loose, rattling and shaking as it opened or closed. Just inside the door was a little square of concrete. On entering the dojo, you had to remove your shoes at that little postage stamp of concrete before stepping up onto the polished wood of the floor. I had come to the dojo with Klaus, a German friend, and we both balanced awkwardly, bumping each other, blocking the doorway. By the side of the door was a cupboard with shelves for the shoes, but often the cupboard was full, and you had to leave your footwear in an untidy pile in the porchway, to be kicked and trampled by incoming and outgoing students. Kicked and trampled, but never stolen.

Once shoeless and up onto the wooden floor, Klaus

---

* Nakayama sensei now holds the eighth degree black belt.

bowed, and I copied awkwardly. The doorway led directly into the office, small, with three desks jammed together, warm and slightly smelly from an old fashioned kerosene stove, on the top of which bubbled a kettle. A secretary occupied one desk, Takagi sensei, the director, occupied another, while the third desk was occupied by one of that day's instructors. Despite the superb quality of the instruction, monthly fees amounted to only a few dollars, and the association was very poor financially. The building was owned by a small movie company, and from the office led stairs to the company's upstairs cutting rooms.

Klaus had been practicing for several months, and had gained the sixth kyu grade, entitling him to wear a green belt. He was at ease, but I was not. He led me over to Takagi sensei's desk, and I bowed again. The sensei smiled. Klaus told him that I wanted to join, and that I was sure. Takagi sensei told me to sit down and told Klaus to go and practice. He asked many questions, in short, clipped English sentences. At that time I could understand no Japanese. He asked what I had been doing before I came to Japan, and when I told him he was impressed, for I had just finished a one-and-a-half-year expedition to the high Arctic, and I boasted a little, for at the age of twenty-two, this had been my third Arctic expedition.

Takagi sensei always took great interest in the welfare and character of his foreign students. He told me once that these young men were to interpret Karate and spread it throughout the world, and he wanted to insure that they did not learn a mistaken philosophy. We passed by his desk every day, and he knew who practiced, who behaved well, who was sincere. We talked for an hour, and he himself filled out my application for enrollment.

I was now a member of the Japan Karate Association, and my headquarters dojo was Yotsuya. Tuition was two thousand yen a month (about six dollars), and for this I could train every day except Thursday, when the dojo was closed to beginners.

I bought a karategi, a white uniform of cotton material, with loose pants that were held up by a drawstring, and a short jacket that was held around the middle by a white belt. For good reason, the karategi is lighter than the uniform used for Judo. It doesn't get yanked and pulled around that much, so it doesn't need the extra strength, and moreover, the heaviness of the judogi might slow down the Karateka, for even in midwinter, the Karateka sweats profusely while training, and needs only a light, very loose covering.

Outside, three tapered posts were embedded in the ground, bound at the top with pads of woven straw rope, or with the more modern pads of canvas and rubber. These were called makiwara, and were targets for punching and striking.

Hips low, bodies turning with each punch, three young black belts struck at the boards, in time with each other, following the sharply exhaled count of the leader. Thump, thump, thump . . . the smack of fist on board and the chant-like counting seemed to punctuate the minutes left before my first formal lesson in Karate, and I changed for it in the small and clothes-jumbled dressing room. Klaus had left by now, and I knew nobody. The room was filling, and a few of the students nodded toward me. Those with the black, high-collared Prussian student uniforms bowed and greeted each other with ostentatious and vigorous formality. People laughed and joked, but there was no back-slapping horseplay. Clothes were piled on top of clothes on the floor, or on the old-fashioned coat pegs of which there were far too few. Wallets were left in pockets, for there was no pilfering here, and no fear of it.

I tied the white belt around me and stepped into the dojo itself, bowing as I entered, for this much I had learned long ago in Cheltenham, England, while practicing Judo at a YMCA.

Once on the dojo floor, the other students did exercises to loosen and stretch muscles and tendons. A senior student, one of the black belts, barked an order and everybody hurried into kneeling lines. The teacher, a third degree black belt, entered the dojo and knelt in front of us. At a second order, all fidgeting ceased. Silence. Stillness. At the furthest end of the rear line, I was conscious of the dull dark polish of the wooden floor, and above, the high dusty ceiling, and on the wall to one side, up and down lines of bold black Japanese letters, but these were on the edges of my vision, for I looked straight ahead like the others. To the front was the red circle of the sun flag, and a photograph of Funakoshi sensei. Silence. I tried to draw myself into it, but it excluded me, and I held my breath lest I should make a noise, and hovered uncertain on the edge of it, for I did not know, and would not know for some time, exactly what we were doing. The senior shouted another order, and we all bowed to the front, and then to the teacher, who in turn bowed to us.

As the class started, a young teacher came to take me and two other beginners, both Japanese, to one side. First he showed us how to form a fist, folding in the fingers tightly, then binding them strong with the thumb. When the fist was opened, the palm of the hand was white, so tightly was the fist formed. Then we began to learn how to stand naturally, feet shoulder-width apart. This is called "shizentai"—natural stance—so utterly simple, and yet we beginners could not stand naturally, for nervousness and eagerness made our shoulders tight, and threw weight back against the curve of our spines.

Now the other students were moving across the floor in lines, blocking, kicking and punching. My eyes strayed, and the young teacher spoke sharply.

From the natural stance, he showed us the "zen-kutsu dachi," the forward stance, accompanied in this instance by a downward sweep of the arm, fist closed. This movement is called "gedan barai"—down-sweeping block. Oh, in the years that have followed, how many times have I practiced this movement, and still not perfected it? Speaking but a few words of English, the young teacher, whose name was Sasaki, and who later was to become my friend, directed our limbs and bodies by pushing and nudging.

. . . Zenkutsu dachi . . . forward, strong, long, with feet double-shoulder-width apart, forward knee over the forward toe, great strength in the muscles of thigh and ankle, lower abdomen slightly tensed, shoulders down, eyes facing the direction of the "enemy."

The stance of the Karateka roots him to the earth at the moment of impact. For a split second in time he is a statue, like a stone from the earth, and then, after the blow is delivered, he relaxes, and his body recoils in preparation for the next move, taking more of the water form of which most of his body is made up. Stone, earth, water. Movement and non-movement.

In this first hour of formal Karate, I had begun to learn that the stances of the Karateka, in their ultimate simplicity, were in fact the most difficult thing. They were "kihon"—basic. They were the strength and balance of the fighter, of the man at peace, of the man in readiness. Upon the stance was built all technique. And also, in this first lesson I learned that despite my muscular, one hundred and ninety-five pound body, I was weak because my stance was weak.

The hour flew, and we were kneeling again, and once more the silence enveloped us, and we tried to push out the murmuring of the city. At a command, the senior student led the kneeling lines in a powerfully chanted oath, the oath of the Karateka. I did not understand it at that time, for it was in Japanese of course, but I knew that it was of importance. The students were intense, straight-staring, and in the rhythm and power of the chant I felt the strong and poetic language of the Japanese male. Later, when the language began to unfold to me, the oath took on a beauty I cannot express in English.

> *. . . The senior, at the head of the line . . .*
> *"Dojo kun!" (morals of the dojo)*
> *"Hitotsu! Jinkaku kansei ni tsutomuru koto!"*
> *(One! To strive for the perfection of character!)*
> *"Hitotsu! Makoto no michi o mamoru koto!"*
> *(One! To defend the paths of truth!)*
> *"Hitotsu! Doryoku no seishin o yashinau koto!"*
> *(One! To foster the spirit of effort!)*
> *"Hitotsu! Reigi o omonzuru koto!"*
> *(One! To honor the principles of etiquette!)*
> *"Hitotsu! Kekki no yu o imashimuru koto!"*
> *(One! To guard against impetuous courage!)*

The oath was always chanted with strength, never mumbled in insincerity. Just as movements would become automatic and reflexes conditioned, the simple truths of the oath would also penetrate the mind of the participant.

Again, we bowed to the front, where Funakoshi sensei's stern image looked down on us, and then we bowed again to the teacher, with spoken thanks. The teacher rose and walked out. Conversation erupted with his departure, animated, jovial, enthusiastic. Now the students were beginning to return to the world of self. But this sudden eruption subsided gradually, while students began to practice individually, and some to spar with each other. Others went out to fetch buckets of water and cloths, and within five minutes the entire floor had been washed clean, ready for the next class. I watched the sparring, or free fighting, for a little while before bowing out of the dojo.

∽ chapter two ∽

Once outside the dojo, I walked, knowing that I had
begun a very definite new chapter in my life, and in the
understanding of this, I found myself more aware of
the sounds and colors around me, some familiar—cars
and buses and diesel fumes and trucks—hurrying housewives with their hair in scarves and shopping baskets in
hand—ugly and impatient machinery noises of cars rev-
ving at stop lights, and the monotonous thump and huff
of a smoke-snorting pile driver. I moved in a world of
sight and sound, my skin still tingling from the cold
shower after the workout, and my ears and eyes receiving all these things which were familiar, and others
which were unfamiliar—like the squeaky warble of a
noodle vendor's trumpet, as he pushed his steaming cart
along the street—delivery boys in white jackets, balanc-
ing tray upon tray of hot food on one hand as they
steered bicycles with the other—the unexpected clip-
clop of wooden clogs on the sidewalk as a student strode
down the street, the top of his high black uniform un-
done, hair cropped close to the skull, karategi slung non-
chalantly over his shoulder by the neatly tied belt.

Beginning to study had brought upon me the realization that I was indeed in Japan, a country that I had read and thought about for so long. I stopped at a building site and watched the bow-legged, baggy-panted construction workers scramble like monkeys over the spiderweb trellises of rope and poles that they put up around the buildings they worked on. They were muscular, brown little men, with split-toed, rubber-soled shoes, festoons of rope pieces hanging from their belts, sweat bands of tied hand towels around their foreheads and woolen cummerbunds around their waists. One of them, stripped to the waist, had an intricate dragon tattoo that completely covered one bicep and shoulder— later I was to read that this tattoo was the mark of a member of a gang society, a yakuza.

I stopped, too, to gaze in fascination at the stalls of a fishmonger, to admire the delicate pallid red of the snappers, the steely wash and blue banding of mackerel, the gray of the flatfishes' upper sides and the astonishing white of their undersides, the mottled spots of squid, the boiled red of octopus and spiny lobsters, the silver sheen of herring and anchovy. There were fish that I had never seen before, all set around with a dozen kinds of shellfish, and, on a block, a huge red cube of whale-meat. The fishmonger was shouting boisterously, chiding and cajoling hesitant housewives, all the while working with the fast, deft strokes of his filleting knife. Sea smells, pervading the fumes of the street.

After a meal of curried rice, chosen and ordered by number from a small display window of plastic imitation meals, I made my way back to the Kodokan, where I rented a room on the third floor. The Kodokan is the headquarters of world Judo. It is a large modern building, with several dojos, offices, and rooms that are rented to students and visitors.

·14·

Judo had been my passion since I was fourteen and had joined a YMCA club in Cheltenham, England. In coming to Japan to learn the arts of the warrior, Karate and Judo had been most prominent in my mind. Of Judo, I knew a little, and had known where to come, but at the time I had studied in England, in the late fifties, there had been perhaps one Karate teacher, only one, in the entire country. Now, twenty years later, this has changed, and Britain has dozens of Karate teachers.

In coming to Japan, with a definite purpose in mind, I had gone first to the center of Judo, the Kodokan, and had been surprised, and pleased, that I could move out of the hotel room on the very first day, stay with a friend (Klaus, the German, whose brother I had gone to school with) for a few days, then move into my austere room in the Kodokan.

The room overlooked the Korakuen amusement park, and the din of loud music and fun machines rattled at my window. Disillusion. Shattered dreams of quiet dojos, wind in willow trees, sounds of trickling water in bamboo pipes. In the street, traffic roared, and a few hundred yards away the subway burst at frequent intervals, rumbling and rushing like an angry bear from its cave, to an open, raised subway station. Very convenient for getting to downtown Tokyo, but not for the fostering of dreams.

Alas, the room was Western and lacked the "tatami" or thick straw mats that the Japanese used in their homes. In the practice of Judo, I had two choices: either to receive instruction in the small, tatami-floored dojo that was set aside especially for foreigners, and only for foreigners, or to go upstairs to the big hall which was used by everybody for free practice. But I needed instruction. Going up to the big hall only meant that I would be a target for the young Japanese black belts who wanted to use a hefty foreigner to toss around. This was all very well, good perhaps to teach me humility, but when I went to Japan I weighed a hundred and ninety-five pounds, was very strong, knew a smattering of Judo and wrestling, and had just come off a year and a half of expedition life that made me as fit and determined as the next man. Second dans (degree black belts) tossed me around without mercy. My ankles were a mass of bruises from their hard foot sweeps. But the first dan black belts, the Japanese that is, were smaller than I, and I gave them a lot of trouble, often dragging them down to the ground and squeezing them into submission with the crudest of techniques. I wasn't learning Judo—"The Gentle Way"—I was beginning to learn how to make it awkward for other people to throw me.

One evening, in the foreigners' dojo, just after I had fought and defeated a smaller man with a hold, a big Westerner took me aside and told me to demonstrate my forward rolling breakfalls. He wore a black belt, and I obeyed him. He watched for a while and then went over to speak to the Japanese teacher. Together they came back to me, and the Westerner, an American, said I should practice my breakfalls for a month, because they were bad. Breakfalls are the first thing a Judoka (practitioner of Judo) learns. What the man was telling me was that I knew nothing, even though I had just defeated a black belt. The American was kind, and told me that if I did not develop good basic technique now, I would never shake off my bad habits and style. He was right, but the Japanese teachers in the foreigners' dojo did not seem to care, and I did not know enough to seek out my own instruction and discipline.

A little while later, while drying myself off in the changing rooms after Judo, a burly Japanese man of about forty came over and talked to me. He said he taught Judo in Sapporo, Hokkaido, and asked me where I was from.

"I am from Britain," I said.

He smiled. "Britain. Oh, good." He pointed at my shoulders. "You are very strong." He pointed to the white belt I had been wearing* and then pointed back at my shoulders. "You come to Hokkaido. In six months I teach you good Judo and you get shodan."

I flushed with pride and asked many questions. Shodan? A first degree black belt in six months? That was worth thinking about! He gave me his card, and I thanked him and said that I would think it over.

I continued practicing both Judo and Karate, and stewed this over in my mind for a month. Then, one morning at the Karate dojo, I asked Takagi sensei how long it would take me to get a black belt. He looked up at me, stood, went from behind the desk and opened up the big cupboard where they kept the uniforms. He took out a brand-new black belt.

"You want this?"

I faltered, knowing that I had said something wrong. Then he threw the belt at me.

"Take this black belt and go back to your country."

I had to backpedal, to explain. The Japanese do not refer to the black belt as such. They do not say "first degree black belt" as we do, conscious more of the outward symbol than of the intrinsic standard of skill. The Japanese say "shodan" or "nidan" and so on, meaning "first step," "second step," etc. Indeed, Judo and Karate men outside of Japan have adopted the Japanese vocabulary, for they have recognized this.

_____
* In European Judo, you start with a white belt, then go to yellow, orange, green, blue, brown and finally to black. In Japan the first three grades wear white belt, then for the next three grades they wear brown.

And yet, when Japanese dojo friends were posing for group pictures, they often tried to get me to wear a black belt, just for the photograph, but after that little lesson from Takagi sensei I resolved never to put on a black belt unless I won the grade, and I never asked again about a black belt.

By the end of the second month I had fixed a routine of living. Karate in the mornings. Lunch in the Yotsuya district, usually at a Chinese restaurant with Klaus and his friend Werner, or at a noodle shop with some Japanese friends. After lunch, a leisurely cup of coffee and half an hour of music and conversation. In the afternoons I went to practice Judo at Sophia University, the international university which was just the other side of the railway line and a short walk from the Karate dojo. The club captain had invited me to train with the Sophia University Judo Club every day, and I did, for it was smaller and more personal (and for me, a beginner, more instructive) than the Kodokan. In the evenings, I went back to the Kodokan and practiced there.

But things were not going well. Crowded Tokyo magnified my loneliness. In language and life-style, I lived apart from the people. I had not yet truly found a place to belong. Coming off an Arctic expedition, with its close and isolated companionship, did not equip me emotionally for dealing with huge, alien crowds, or for the many people I had to know, greet and be friendly with.

I had a girl friend in Australia who wanted me to go there. My family wanted me to go back to England. I was lonely. Should I give up this dream? It was not giving me the sense of place and purpose that I thought it would. But no, I decided to wait another few months at least.

·18·

And so the time was right to meet a man who would largely change my way of life. In fact I had already met him on the dojo mats. He was the big American who criticized my Judo breakfalls. Donn Draeger, sixth degree black belt in Judo, sixth degree black belt in Jojitsu (stick fighting) and black belt rank in a dozen other martial arts. Tall, extremely muscular, upright, with piercing eyes and a quick, easy laugh, Donn is a most impressive man. He is also a very gentle man, quick to help a student, tell a joke when needed, help out a friend or a stranger.

I had just come in the front entrance of the Kodokan when I spotted an old acquaintance from Montreal, Doug Rogers (later to win a silver medal for Canada in Judo at the 1964 Olympics). Doug was talking to Donn Draeger, and I noticed something. Two burly Meiji University students passed the two foreigners, but before they went by Donn they bowed and greeted him as they would a Japanese Judo sensei. I stopped to talk with Doug and Donn, and after Doug rushed off to catch a train, Donn asked me how things were going. He listened with sympathy.

"Well, look here, Nic, we've got a house in Ichigaya, just a couple of stations down the line from Suidobashi. There's a room there for you if you'd care to join us. We're all here to study—Judo, Karate, stick and so on —so you'd be in with guys you could talk to. Look, drop by this evening, and take a look at the place."

That evening I found my way up to the big old wooden house on Ichigaya hill. By a miracle, or a series of miracles, the house had escaped the fire bomb raids of the Second World War. It was one of the few Meiji period houses left in Tokyo, built about a hundred years ago when wood was more plentiful, when houses could be more spacious. Its basic design was Japanese, two-storied, with traditional rooms, sliding screens and doors, massive oaken beams and pillars, polished wooden corridors, alcoves hung with scrolls. The sitting room, however, was Western in design. It was during the period of the Emperor Meiji that the first real influx of Western thought and design invaded Japan, and it was evidenced here by this large, cold, dusty room with its Victorian furniture, European windows, heavy drapes and shelves. It was used as a gymnasium rather than as a place to sit, for everybody preferred the comfort and airiness of tatami mats and sliding paper screens—the shoji—that filtered the light and gave it a definite quality of softness and gentleness, of privacy without imprisonment.

Donn greeted me and made tea, in the Japanese way, with an iron kettle, in his room. He served the tea in precious bowls, which were stored carefully in little wooden chests. On a low Japanese desk were his typewriter and an unfinished manuscript. He has written many books, and is reckoned by most to be the foremost Western exponent of martial arts. He had changed, as most Japanese men do, from his Western street clothes into a warm, comfortable garment called a "tanzen," a man's winter kimono, quilted, tied with a wide silk belt. In the alcove was a hanging scroll and a flower arrangement, and on the walls were racks of fighting sticks, clubs, training swords, and other close-combat weapons. We talked about martial arts, and about the best way for me, a beginner, to go about learning and living them. I decided to accept Donn's offer, and took a room in the house, sharing the facilities, responsibilities and rent. I moved my kit bag up from the Kodokan the next day.

Now, this was more as I had imagined living in Japan would be. I had the biggest room. It had no less than ten mats, and three sides of the room were windows, glass on the outside, and then a few inches of space, and then screens of wood and rice paper. I bought a low Japanese table, a Japanese mattress and quilts. I even bought a tanzen and a silk sash to tie it with. Now, in the evenings, I could retreat into the austere but airy beauty of my room, sip the roasted tea that I came to love, read a book, write a letter, think a thought. The hill was quiet, and the narrow lane that led up past the house was too narrow for any but the crazy kamikaze taxi drivers to drive fast on. The city whispered. It did not roar as it had in the Kodokan. In walking from the station I passed little carp ponds where Japanese men and boys went to pay their money, hire a bamboo rod, line, hook and bait, and then sit elbow to elbow and catch carp and goldfish to take home in plastic bags of water. I passed a few small bars, two coffee shops, a cake shop, greengrocer, fishmonger and butcher. The shop people began to recognize me and to call out the greetings of the day, and as I walked from the station I began to feel, if not at home, then at least in place.

The house was fine. It had a ponderous, somber grace. It faced out onto a garden landscaped with trees and stones and a little pond. It was surrounded by a high wall, over which the boughs of cherry and plum trees bent with artful intimacy. We even had a large, fat, resident toad, who sat under the house or by the pond, and looked upon life with the patience and mellowness of Buddha.

It took me only twenty minutes to walk from the house in Ichigaya to the Karate dojo in Yotsuya, and not much longer to catch a train to Suidobashi, just a short walk from the Kodokan.

I lived upstairs, as did Donn and another American

called Bill Fuller. Bill was a second dan black belt in Judo and in Jojitsu, stick fighting. Downstairs were a couple of rooms that were used largely by transient martial arts students: Canadian, American, European, British.

We were all Budoka. It wasn't until I moved into the house on the hill that the word "Budoka" came to mean anything to me. Budo is the way of the warrior, and so "Budoka" is a student of martial arts, whether it be Judo, Karate, Aikido, Kendo, Kempo, Jojitsu or what-have-you. We are an elitist group. We are international. We fight and argue among ourselves but try to present a united front to the outside. But most significant, the Budoka is a doer and a thinker. The Budoka is not a watcher, a spectator. In the house on the hill we Budoka shared tales, discussed training methods, argued. Donn Draeger was our "sempai"—our senior. I was by far the most junior in skills and, by a few years, in age, and Donn influenced me profoundly.

My own background was not pro-Japanese. My deep adolescent interest in things Japanese horrified my family. The British too are an island people, often closed in their thoughts, and they had been soundly and well beaten by the Japanese. Britain, in my youth, still resounded with tales of tortured prisoners, beheadings, jungle railways. Donn showed me a different side of the coin. He had fought in the Pacific war, seen friends die beside him on the beaches of Iwo Jima, faced and killed Japanese under circumstances of hate, and yet here was a man who loved and respected the Japanese, who understood that gentleness was the way of the warrior. Bigotry is left to those people on the fringe.

Once ensconced in my room, and at home there, I could take the first positive step toward a private and inward fight. At a nearby lumberyard I had a six-foot post cut and shaped for me. At the bottom it was four inches wide and four inches thick, but the back was cut away so that it tapered to only three quarters of an inch in thickness at the top. This tapering gave the board a little springiness, not too much, but enough to give a little under strong pressure. In a corner of the garden, hidden by walls and trees, I embedded the post in the ground, bracing it with large buried stones. Now the tip of the post came just above the tip of my solar plexus, and to this tip I secured a pad of hard rubber and canvas. This post and pad is an essential training device of a Karateka. It is called a makiwara. The traditional pad was plaited from straw rope, but it was some months afterwards that a teacher taught me how to make one. The straw rope pad is much rougher on the hands, and quickly develops calluses.

Over the following months I directed millions of foot-pounds of energy at this target. The canvas became flecked and mottled with blood when I punched poorly and grazed my knuckles. I used the makiwara every day. It was (and still is) a deeply personal fight. Nobody could watch me, see my little victories and defeats.

From the mind came power. In essence it was the mind that willed the leg to thrust, ankle to tense and root the foot to the ground, the hips to pivot, the punching arm to lance out and tense, twisting just on impact, while at the same time the opposite hand clenched and drew into the opposite side, and at impact the air was forced out of the body as all the muscles of thorax and abdomen tensed. For a given portion of each day, the makiwara target became the object of concentration, of focus. It was stationary, passive. It had dignity. In facing the makiwara, I had to become composed, just as later I would have to learn composure before a human opponent. My body was like a spring. I worked fifty

punches on the right side, fifty on the left side, fifty right, fifty left. Breath inhaled as the spring coiled, exhaled as the fist contacted, smacking the board back. Thwock! Even in the winter I sweated at the makiwara. Each victory over my body, in delivering a good punch or a strike, was yet still a victory for the makiwara. It absorbed good and bad blows with impunity, and took its toll from me in skin, blood, and wrist sprains. I faced it and worked. From the punching exercises I would shift stance and strike with the edge of my open hand—the "shuto" or knife hand. I would also strike with the edge of the closed fist, and with the back of the fist. I also tied a pad of canvas and sand to a stout old plum tree and used that for kicking. The muscles of the leg are so powerful that even a resilient makiwara could break with a well-focused kick.

The makiwara demanded a great deal of me, to stand thus alone, sometimes in the rain, sweating and striking, thinking and non-thinking, watching my form and trying to muster strength, speed and focus, hitting the pad so many times. Yet, though demanding, I found great peace in it. The target was simple, the conflict between nerve, bone, muscle, sinew, mind, rubber, wood and earth. Through my conflict with the makiwara I brought slow change to myself and without humiliation or change to the target. This training was not a mere pounding of fists, it was an exercise of concentration and release, it had rhythm, and the gradual building of awareness in timing, distance and strength.

In the Karate dojo in Yotsuya, there was a large sign in flowing black characters, the words of Gichin Funakoshi: "The ultimate aim of the art of Karate lies not in victory or defeat, but in the perfection of the character of its participants."

In the matter of toughening the hands, I heard

foolish advice at the Karate dojo; never from a teacher, mark you, but from a few of the black belts, especially the hard-headed, shaven-headed university toughs. It was said that the beginner should gather courage and smash his fist into a concrete wall. By doing this he would break the knuckles of his fists, and these would, in a few months, fuse into a hard, strong knot. That some beginners did this was evidenced by the blood on the wall outside the dojo. When I was told to do this I called the man a fool. You don't have to be a doctor to know that this could create bad problems. Many times I saw young men with greatly enlarged knuckles that looked like awesome weapons, but which were, in fact, soft and tender even after a couple of years, for each hard strike renewed the old and serious injury to the tissues. To me my hands would never be degraded to a mere weapon. I would eventually develop to a point where I could decide, within myself, to give them weapon-nature, but then immediately afterward to return them to their other natures. I wanted to be strong, but I still wanted to be able to use a microscope, caress, type, and perhaps to play the guitar. And so, over a period of time, I built strength in my hands and wrists, and ignored foolish advice.

However, our garden wall was built of cement blocks, supported by reinforced concrete posts. When my hands grew stronger I began to strike at the concrete, and on one of the posts, at neck height, I wore a shallow white patch by repeatedly striking it with "shuto," knife hand (what outsiders call a "Karate chop"). To punch at the concrete with my clenched fist took more time and a lot of courage, but eventually I could do it. I had first to learn that strength was in the mind, and that if I wanted to avoid injury, I had to convince myself that my hand had become weapon steel, and not mere flesh and bone.

Months passed, and many things happened. I fell in love, began to learn the Japanese language, made friends, traveled a little in the country. But I had become stuck on a plateau, despite many hours of hard training. I began to feel very tired, and to ache each morning with minor bruises and sprains. Neither in Karate nor Judo was I progressing.

As I came into the dojo one morning, carrying the twin bundles of Karate and Judo uniforms, Takagi sensei stopped me, and pointed to them.

"What is that?" He was asking about the judogi, and I was surprised, knowing full well that nearly all of our teachers held black belt grades in both Judo and Kendo (fencing). I answered simply in Japanese.

"Sensei, it is my judogi. After the Karate lesson I will go and practice Judo."

"A hunter who chases two rabbits at the same time will catch neither of them. Make up your mind. Do you wish to learn Judo or Karate? You are a beginner in both. They oppose each other within you. Your spirit is pulled in two ways. I have watched you. Gradually you are losing strength instead of gaining it. Judo is good, but you cannot learn both, Karate and Judo are too different. You do not progress here, and I think that you do not progress at the Kodokan either. Make up your mind."

And then, looking back to the letter he was writing, he said no more to me.

Even though I loved it, I quit Judo, and devoted myself mainly to Karate. Oh, once in a while I would take my judogi and go to the Kodokan to fight on the mats, but no longer did I train at Judo. Up to this point I had been training six hours a day, and was losing weight and strength, but now, training only three hours, but with great concentration, I felt much better, and all the lingering aches and minor injuries healed.

While I was practicing one day, Takagi sensei called me over to the dojo door. I bowed out.

"You still have not taken the examination for eighth kyu. Why is this?" The eighth and seventh kyu still only entitled the holder to wear a white belt.

"Eighth kyu has no meaning for me," I answered.

He became very angry and shouted at me. "Each rank in Karate has meaning, and each Karateka must grasp the meaning of those ranks. You will open your eyes before you sit up and raise your head, crawl before you walk, and walk before you run. You must take the examination on Sunday."

"Yes!" I bowed and shouted the reply. A Karateka does not answer his teacher with a small and weak voice.

"Go now and practice the form. You are too high and weak in the hips."

"Yes!" I shouted.

Other more senior students glanced at me and smiled. It was amusing, and perhaps gratifying to see the Britisher shouting out his answers in Japanese.

"Nic! Do not stand and be lazy, get into the dojo!" This time it was Sasaki, my teacher, senior and friend. He was merciless.

I took the examination on the Sunday, and not only passed, but jumped to seventh kyu grade. I still wore a white belt, but the next step would be to green.

∽ chapter three ∽

Unlike some other styles, our school did not use intricate movements of the hands to baffle opponents in free-fighting. We prefer rather to remain in a fighting stance, moving very little, until the opponent has committed himself to the attack, or until he has shown his weakness. Therefore, the techniques that won more contests than any other were not the spectacular high kicks or difficult strikes, but rather the basic reverse punch and front kick.

I tried then to develop these two techniques strongly, and concentrated on them to the neglect of others. The reverse punch, or "gyaku-zuki," is usually delivered from a front stance, or "zenkutsu-dachi." It is a deep stance, with hips low, and with the leading leg bent so that the leading knee is over the toe of the leading foot. It was the first fighting stance taught at our school. If the left foot is forward, then the punch is delivered with the right fist, and if the right leg is forward, the punch is delivered with the left fist. Delivered properly, it is an extremely fast and powerful blow, a killing blow, for in its focus, all the strength of the body is mustered.

The front kick, or "mae-geri," is also usually delivered from the "zenkutsu-dachi" stance. The kick is fast, too quick for the foot to be caught. The opponent is struck by the ball of the foot, anywhere from the shin to the face. It is the first kick taught to a Karateka.

While other students got their seniors to tutor them after formal classes in the styles and forms, or spent time sparring, I kept repeating the same two moves, usually against the makiwara at the dojo. I did not ask for help, but senior students often came and corrected my stance, or explained how I should breathe, and concentrate power in the lower abdomen.

Calluses formed on my hands, especially on the first two knuckles of my fists, and like all new Karateka, I was proud of them. On trains, if I got a seat, I sat with my fists clenched loosely in front of me, childishly displaying the signs of the art I was learning. Awareness had come into my fists, and I became conscious of their strength. I broke boards and tiles, and all that kind of nonsense. This awareness in my hands was perhaps the first signs of acquiring Karate. Later, the awareness would shift, and eventually, I hope, become all-encompassing. But the fists were the seeds of it.

In order to understand Japanese feelings, and Japanese strength, you must realize that a sense of place within a group is essential to the Japanese well-being. This can be misunderstood. Some Westerners have thought that the Japanese seek this sense of place, or group identity, out of weakness. False. The Japanese nature is extremely loyal, and loyalty only to oneself or one's family would rot the soul with its selfishness.

The Karate dojo gave even me, a foreigner, a sense of belonging. I began to make friends there, both for-

eign and Japanese, and I built up the vital relationship of "kohai" and "sempai"—junior and senior. From his sempai the Karateka learns spirit. If the teacher is the driver, and the class the engine, then the sempai are the rods that force the rest of the engine to work. They shouted and cursed, insulted and encouraged, praised and scorned. When a student faltered, his seniors would push, slap, or kick him, somehow goading him on just a little further than he himself thought he could go.

One day, when we were in class, and advancing across the floor at the command of the teacher, kicking and punching, the teacher told us to move further, faster, deeper with each move. Already we were low and deep, and my legs were trembling with fatigue. I got ready for the command to move, and when it came, I moved as far and as fast as I thought I could. With a force that almost lifted me off the ground, I took a kick in the seat of my pants. Irate, I turned around. It was my sempai, Okuda.

"Move!" he said.

"You!" shouted the teacher. "Face front! Concentrate! Drive off your back leg! If you are tired go and lie down. This is a Karate class!"

Somewhere I found a little more speed and range, though for the next ten minutes I received a few more gentle reminders in the arse.

Our sempai showed us that to give up was the worse disgrace, even though to lose was sometimes inevitable. They were both friends and tyrants. Later, as we rose in rank, we would pass the spirit on to others.

The dojo forced discipline onto me, often a harsh discipline. Once at a morning class while we stood in a ready stance, listening to the teacher's instructions, I yawned. The teacher walked over to me, stopped, looked me in the eyes and gave me a stinging slap

across the face. I knew enough to keep on staring ahead.

"Nicol-san, are you awake now?"

"Yes!" I shouted.

"Good." He walked back to his place and went on teaching the class.

Yet, had I wanted to, I was always free to quit. We learned to behave with politeness and respect, we learned to go further with ourselves than we thought we could. We did menial things. After each class the students closest to the door would rush out to get buckets of water and cloths. As many as could grabbed a cloth, dampened it in the water and placed it on the floor. Both hands were placed on the cloth, and with his buttocks high and his body almost in a "push-up" position, the washer ran the width of the dojo, cleaning a foot-wide swath. We raced each other across the dojo in this way, thus strengthening hips, legs and arms, and sometimes crashing into each other, laughing and panting.

This task was never omitted, and nobody was ever ordered or asked to do it. A few, especially Westerners, dodged it, but the teachers and sempai always knew, and although they said nothing, the result of their observations would come out in the quality of individual instruction. Slackers, dodgers, and those with poor spirit were ignored on the dojo floor.

The dojo gave me friends, seniors, teachers, a sense of belonging and a sense of responsibility. On the lapel of my old tweed jacket I wore the red circle badge, small and unobtrusive, yet signifying my affiliation to the JKA. On my hands I carried the marks of a Karate man. We were urged to walk and sit straight, and to carry ourselves with dignity.

When I was out with dojo friends, drinking or eating, they always took care to try to teach me the polite way to do things. I was taught to raise my sake cup when somebody poured for me, and to return the courtesy of pouring. I was scolded for sticking my chopsticks in the rice, for blowing my nose (even with a tissue) in public, and for a dozen other things. My sempai were concerned for my education.

At lunch time one day, a foreign student stood at the inner door of the dojo, eating a banana. Enoeda sensei, tall, powerful, and a fourth dan, stormed out of the office, grabbed him by the neck and led him to a chair by a table.

"You sit!" Enoeda was learning English. "Eat. No stand. Stand and eat no good. Understand?"

The student grinned sheepishly and did as he was told. Enoeda sensei stormed out again, and I heard him being ribbed for his English by the other teachers.

"They are like children," he said, "and it is our responsibility to teach them etiquette."

A few minutes later the secretary brought the student some tea.

On another occasion, Sasaki was walking past Shibuya station, one of the most crowded places in Tokyo, when he saw one of our students, a Swiss who had hitched his way to Japan, begging outside the main subway exit. The Swiss had sometimes expounded his theories that begging was good for the soul, for the humility of man. In Tokyo, it also earned his food, lodging, beer and clothes. Sasaki stopped in front of the Swiss.

"Get up!"

Sasaki's fierce glare silenced the beginnings of a protest.

"Come with me!"

The Swiss followed Sasaki to a nearby restaurant. Sasaki ordered food for them both. When they had finished eating Sasaki warned him that if he was in such

bad trouble that he had to beg, then he should come to the dojo and tell us. If not, he could stay away from the dojo and beware for his health if ever one of the seniors saw him begging again. The Swiss left very soon after and went to India.

Although Karate is the ultimate in unarmed violence, the responsibility and trust we felt for each other, and the high standards of politeness maintained in the dojo, made it a paradoxically gentle art. With only one Karateka did I have an unpleasant relationship, and at that time I wore a white belt, and had not proved myself.

We foreign students nicknamed him "Bullet Head." He was a member of the Takushoku University Karate team, a group known for its fanatical dedication. He loathed foreigners and bullied us unmercifully on the dojo floor. I guessed his politics to be ultra right-wing. Off the dojo floor, if he spoke to us at all, it was in sneering tones. As we were changing one day, Bullet Head jabbed his finger at my shoulder, saying that all the muscle there did me no good, and that although I might be strong, I couldn't be fast. Had the jibe come from one of my sempai, I would have taken it well, for there was some truth in it, but coming from this bully I took it with a grudge, and that was how he wanted it.

White belts very rarely did any free fighting, or sparring, because their control is bad, and their blows would not be so well focused that the strength would be delivered outside the sparring partner's body, but might actually strike him. We did not wear padded, protective clothing, or pillow-like gloves, and a wild and uncontrolled fist or foot could break a nose or a rib. However, at times, the teachers would line us up against the brown and black belts, who, presumably, could block our dangerously awkward moves, and yet could deliver their counter attacks without causing injury. To actually strike a partner is a foul. This kind of training was more for the benefit of the higher grades.

It was my bad luck, or fate, to be faced with Bullet Head. Black belt against white belt. He moved around me, repeatedly slapping my face, taunting me, saying that I was too slow and clumsy. In the meantime he blocked my ill-timed blows, and snapped his focused punches, kicks and strikes to my head and body. The true Karate attacks did not hurt, for they were controlled, and did not penetrate, but the slaps stung. A red haze of anger formed around the edges of my vision, and with a bellow, probably an Anglo-Saxon expletive, I charged into him, seized him by the crotch and shoulder, lifted him up to my head height, and slammed him down across my knee. Then I lifted him again and ran his head into the wall, once, twice, before the teacher broke it up.

Slightly groggy, Bullet Head got up off the floor where I had dropped him, face blank. The teacher jumped between us and ordered him to finish. Bullet Head bowed, but then glared at me, and I at him. We could both hear the other black belt students and a couple of the younger teachers laughing, not at me, but at him, because he had lost face, and been defeated by a white belt. But that was unfair, because by the time I was twenty-two I had probably been in more street fights, not to mention pro wrestling bouts, than he had been in tournaments. Bullet Head had judged me as a fighter only by his own standards, and by the color of the belt I wore.

The teacher scolded me, and said that I had come to learn Karate, and not to practice wrestling, but I don't think he was at all angry. But I knew that Bullet Head had marked me for a vengeance.

Perhaps because the teachers watched that Bullet Head never sparred with me, but mainly because I avoided him like a plague, he didn't get his chance for a month. But cowardice is an impermanent escape, serving only to compound the fear, and eventually it happened that I was lined up with white and colored belts, one by one stepping out to attack the eight black belts who faced us. We fought them until we were defeated. When I stepped out, I was in front of Bullet Head. We bowed and I adopted the fighting stance, as taught. The shock of that first kick put me back, catching me hard as it did on the hip. I realized that he was kicking hard as he could, with intent to hurt, and aiming at my groin. Why didn't they stop him? I knew too that if I fought him with everything I knew, I might just get him and make the fight more fair, but I was too proud, and determined to fight him as a Karateka. Several kicks came. No slaps this time. I managed to dodge or block, but at last he got me, and pain exploding in my guts passed into numbness and I fell, quite unconscious.

When I came around, dry retching, my friend and sempai Sasaki had pulled me to one side and was leaning over me. The rest of the class were ignoring the incident.

"Nic-san, stand up."

With difficulty, I got up and left the class. A teacher who had been watching took me into the teachers' changing area and told me to take my pants down. He felt my bruised testicles and said I was not ruptured or torn. The pain was still pretty bad though. The sensei grinned.

"Every day, you get a little kick here, and bit by bit you get very strong."

Indignation, anger and shame left me, and I laughed. Surely I had been allowed to answer for my actions. I changed gingerly and watched the rest of the class. Bullet Head was taking a hell of a pounding from Sasaki, and taking it well, and then when Sasaki had finished, another black belt, an experienced second dan, took over. The circle was completed.

~ chapter four ~

Christmas of 1962 had come and gone, and with it
ended an unrequited love affair. At the same time, news
had come that one of my Arctic expedition comrades
had died. My soul demanded a dramatic gesture, and I
set out, and failed, to climb the winter slopes of Mount
Fuji. A tourist attraction in summer, but a deadly lady,
encircled by high winds and slopes of glare ice, with
sub-zero temperatures in winter. I tried and failed,
alone, on two occasions, and although views of the
mountain from an inn in Fuji Yoshida filled me with
awe, the mountain, like the nation and the girl I had
lost, seemed to me to be an enigma—precise in her
beauty, seemingly cold, and yet with a fire in her belly.

For a week or so I trained little and drank much,
but then the knowledge of my own foolishness gave me
greater incentive to follow the Karate path.

My stances were becoming deeper and stronger,
blows faster and better focused. My three sempai, Sasaki, Seto and Okuda were encouraging me. At that
time, Sasaki held the second dan, while the other two

held first. At Sasaki's urging, I had bought iron clogs, with which to practice kicking and strengthen my legs. He also recommended practicing kicks while in a pool or a big Japanese bath. Seto and Okuda taught and encouraged me to learn the kata.

To quote Nakayama sensei—

"Kata are the formal exercises of Karate [and all other martial arts]. They have been passed on from the Chinese origins of Karate, centuries ago, by Karate masters, who also introduced new forms from time to time. Some have been developed fairly recently, and there are at the present time about fifty forms."

It is hard to describe kata, but once seen, the feeling they express is not forgotten (although, as every Karateka will vouch, the movements are forgotten if not practiced regularly). Kata are ritual battles in which the Karateka fights several imaginary opponents. Ritual is the frame on which power and speed are built, and it is through the ritual of the kata that the Karateka strives for perfection.

I had learned, but by no means perfected, two kata, and was now learning a third. These three were all "Heian" kata, numbered simply one to three. To pass the examination for the sixth kyu, the green belt, I had to perform this kata called "Heian sandan" (Heian number three) as well as demonstrate certain basic techniques and fighting skills. Heian sandan is a kata including twenty techniques of blocking, striking, thrusting, stamping, turning, breathing, lunging, and takes roughly forty-five seconds to complete. It has fifteen stance shifts and two shouts which the Karateka call "kiai." Like all kata, it seems to the watcher like a strangely dynamic dance. It is beautiful to watch, for it is a battle without bloodshed or vanquished, and perhaps "dance" is a good word to link to kata.

From the very beginning of history, skill with weapons has been passed down by ritual practice. When the prehistoric or the primitive hunter returned to camp after an encounter with a wild animal or an enemy, he could demonstrate his prowess better by performing than by talking. He would dance, exaggerating and repeating his movements. Young warriors and boys copied the dances, developed them until they were set and ritualized. They were superb training, for in them the warrior could mimic and develop the style, speed and skill of a master.

The Western soldier even performs rituals, giving skill and coordination. He calls them drills, but they are in truth a form of dance.

Before the technical advances of chemicals and machinery took over the battlefield, the sword was the favored weapon of almost all cultures that developed a warrior class. No other weapon was as versatile. The sword could hack, slash, chop, thrust, jab, slap, parry, block or swing. In using the sword the warrior developed tremendous arms, wrists and shoulders. His bones became stronger and his aim truer. This development made the warrior a formidable fighter even without a weapon.

In Okinawa, where the people had been overwhelmed, disarmed and dominated by the Kagoshima invaders, some of the warriors developed fighting skills to substitute their hands, elbows, knees and feet for the weapons of metal and wood they were no longer permitted to carry. The art of unarmed fighting was taught to small groups, in secret, and the ritual forms of kata formed the main part of the training. The power that the old fighters thus developed was enough to kill an opponent even through armor of metal, leather, and lacquered woods.

I believe that when we practice kata, we are somehow touching the warrior ancestry of all humanity. In painting, sculpture, fresco and carving, ritual battles are depicted, not only in Japan and China, but all over the world. Of all the training in Karate, none is more vigorous, demanding and exhilarating than the sincere performance of kata.

Takagi sensei watched and then criticized my performance one morning. "Where is your enemy, Nicol? When you do the kata you are only thinking of yourself. You are not projecting your mind to see the attack that comes to you. Look in the direction of your movements! See the enemy! If you practice hard you will develop a mind that is as calm as still water. Karate is moving Zen, and it is the Zen state that you must strive for."

He never tried to explain what a Zen state was, but much, much later, after trying hard to "see" the enemies, I began to understand. Through concentration on perfection the mind is released, and a great calm, in which the body moves, is achieved. Practice of kata was the best way to know the Zen calm. A decade later, I read of researches in brain wave patterns. It was found that yogi and Zen monks exhibited an alpha wave in meditation. It was also found that Karateka also exhibited this in the "waiting" or "ready" stage of combat, and in the pauses in the kata. Kata is perfection and release.

But like most beginners, I was not concerned then about the Zen state to be achieved by the practice of kata. I wanted to be able to fight. And like all beginners, I tried to make comparisons. What was Karate like against Judo? Or boxing? Or wrestling? Is the Karate way of kicking as strong as that of the Thai boxers? I know now that comparisons are foolish, and miss the whole point of diligent training. If a Karateka were pitted against a boxer and won, it would not prove the superiority of Karate, or even that this particular Kara-teka was better than that particular boxer. A statistical study might give better answers, if you staged a hundred or a thousand contests to the death. But who would volunteer? And which nation would permit such bloodshed? And anyway, what good would it do?

It was a Sunday afternoon, and I had been using my makiwara. Donn was also in the garden, practicing a Chinese form of stick fighting. I stopped to watch him. Donn Draeger used to say that without learning a weapon art, you could not be truly proficient in unarmed combat. Weapons gave you new insights into space, timing, force and territory. The six-foot-long, smoothly polished hardwood staff whirled and spun in his hands, sucking air with a low, moaning sound. Around him, an area described by a wide circle was inviolate. To attempt to attack would be like trying to go through the spinning blades of an aircraft propeller. At times, the stick would dart out of the circle with great speed, and I saw too that it was not just one circle, but circles within circles.

But one move didn't make sense to me. Donn would slide the staff through his left hand, letting it strike out behind him, five feet or so from his own back. It was fast, but I didn't think it looked effective, so asked him.

"Donn, could that back strike do any damage?"

Thud! I had hardly spoken when the staff hit the pillar I was leaning against. It was a thick, oaken pillar, supporting the porch roof. Donn spun around, still wheeling the stick, smiling.

"Sure," he said.

Eight inches from my chest was a half inch dent. Had that seemingly ineffective blow hit me, at least one rib would have broken.

Ever since I started Judo at fourteen, I have heard

people talk disparagingly about other fighting arts. I have done it myself. Certainly I heard enough of it in Japan, yet only very rarely from those who were truly adept in their own art. Part of the trouble is that to simplify instruction, a teacher usually has to tell a student that this or that must be thus or so. But in all studies, once a follower truly begins to delve and wonder he discovers the "ifs" that finally crumble the initial "rule." He might believe, for example, that water flows, is transparent and visible. Yet that, although true, is not the ultimate truth. Water is hard and blue. It is hot vapor. It is white and soft.

I was emerging from a dream, and stretching out in the warm quilts, feeling the sun on my face as it filtered through the screens, enjoying again the faint scent of hay fields from the tatami mats. Earthquake? The building was shuddering. The screens rattled in their sills, and the floor beneath me was moving. Yet the jolts came in a pattern, about one a second. A pile driver nearby? Yet there was no construction going on near us. I pulled on my pants and jeans and went downstairs.

I went into the living room, and there Donn, Bill Fuller and a few other guys were watching a teacher of the Chinese art of Tai chi chuan. His name was Mr. Wong. He weighed about two hundred and fifty pounds, seemed ageless, and he was punching one of the supporting pillars of the house, with his fist moving only a few inches each time. Each blow shook the whole house. I could not believe what I saw. Never had I witnessed such deceptive power. It looked as if he were just thumping the wood, and had anyone asked me, I might have blithely volunteered to take such a blow in my reasonably hard stomach. Had I done so, it would have killed me.

Mr. Wong came to the house to teach Donn Draeger and a select group of high-ranking Budoka. He taught them mainly kata. The Tai chi chuan kata were long, complicated and very slow. It was like a ballet in which each second had been stretched to a minute, as slow as the pushing of a weed through pavement. He performed the kata with enormous dignity and force, and even I, a novice, realized that I was seeing something which, although I could not understand, I had to respect.

The masters of Tai chi chuan are usually advanced in years. In China, people practice the movements for their health in the early morning in the city squares and parks. Despite advancing years, a person can improve skill and power. Westerners often see something like this and scoff—yet how many men of forty in the West are active in a physical sport? How many men of fifty are active? Sixty? Seventy? How many Westerners of eighty years could soundly thrash a man in his twenties? In the Orient, many of the great masters are in their eighties, and still they are formidable.

Mr. Wong was at least fifty, and probably older. His power was fantastic. I saw him hurl Donn Draeger several feet across the room, so hard that his feet were off the floor when he struck the wall. I saw him do the same thing to four very strong men, who stood one behind the other to present a solid, anchored line of over eight hundred pounds. At a single push they all went flying. Then, at one lesson, he allowed me to feel the power of one of his movements, and although he promised to be gentle, I was hurled clean across the room and smashed into the wall. And how? By a simple-looking, one-handed push that looked as harmless as the waking movements of a child. The initial contact of his hand on my chest was indeed gentle, but the accelerating propulsion that followed had to be felt to be believed.

Mr. Wong could take punches or kicks in any part of his body except the face. If he let you, you could kick him square in the groin and he wouldn't even flinch. To demonstrate this power, he once invited ex-heavyweight champion of the world Joe Louis to punch him in the solar plexus. The punch had no effect. He also invited a huge Dutch Karateka to strike him in the stomach, and the Karateka (who Donn said was one of the strongest men he knew) merely hurt his own wrist.

By watching, I could learn little about the techniques of Tai chi chuan, but I learned a lot about not judging from what I thought my eye perceived, or from what my mind had previously assimilated. I felt enormous admiration and respect for this art, but I never took lessons, for I still bore in mind the story of the hunter and the two rabbits.

To be narrow in thought about different arts and different styles was only to foster a weakness. Nakayama sensei, our chief instructor, was certainly not narrow. He had studied many arts, and he had studied in China. Once I asked him if he thought Karate was the best of the unarmed fighting arts. He answered that he thought it was. In that case, I countered, what about Tai chi chuan? Nakayama sensei laughed, and with a smile he said, "For human beings, Karate is the best way. But there are some men who are superhuman, and perhaps a few of the Tai chi sensei are just that."

Knowing the efficiency of Tai chi chuan, why did I not study it? Well, I had put my feet on the Karate path, and there I determined to stay until I had learned what I felt to be enough. Moreover, I believed that the paths of Tai chi chuan and Karate, and indeed, of all the martial arts, led to the same goal. Tranquillity.

∽ chapter five ∽

A Sunday. I walked with a woman called Sonako in a small natural park not far from Meguro station, Tokyo. That morning I had taken the examination for sixth kyu, green belt, and I had passed it. I was no longer a white belt. We walked together, not hand in hand, for some Japanese men become offensive when they see a foreigner walking that way with a Japanese woman.

Unmoving, in a park stream, there were two giant Japanese salamanders, rare creatures that grew to great size and age in pure mountain streams. The salamanders were protected by law, yet were in great and increasing danger from water pollution. These creatures were over three feet long, lying so still. I saw that Sonako didn't shrink from them, but was interested, curious, and for that I liked her even more. I saw her frequently now, at least three times a week, and we were lovers. She liked me a great deal but was distressed at my terrible temper.

May Day, 1963. I was walking from Ichigaya to Yotsuya, on my way to the dojo. The demonstrators were snake-dancing down the street, singing and chanting, all wearing red kerchiefs round their heads or necks, and some with banners. There was a lot of anti-American feeling, and although I am not American, I wore jeans, and I walk with a slight swagger. A few shouted at me—"Yankee go home!"—and jeering words in Japanese. Donn had told me not to go out on the streets where the demonstrators were, but I had ignored him. With one finger raised I indicated that the shouters should disappear up their own rectums, and one of the snake-dancing lines swung close to me, and the next but one swung even closer and bounced me against a wall. Already I was as far over on the sidewalk as I could go, walking in the opposite direction. There were thousands of marchers, hundreds of lines, all with arms linked, line after line. Another line bounced me, and then I got mad, and as another line came close, making as if to bounce me again, I kicked at the inside man and caught him in the stomach. As he faltered, I charged the man next to him, grabbing him by the head and trying to bring his face down to my knee. A crazy thing to do. There was a brief but noisy tumult, and I was prepared to go down berserk. Hundreds of people around me. Police whistles. The lines moved on, and I had no way of knowing if I had hurt anybody, for they were jostled away with the dancing lines, looping, weaving. No other lines came across the sidewalk, and a policeman approached me.

"Where are you going?"
"To the Karate dojo."
"Then hurry up and go, and get off the street."

Anyone who is not cursed with a violent temper can little understand. When the stimulus is great enough you begin to breathe faster, and to tremble, as if in great

fear. Facial muscles twitch, and fists clench. Your guts knot and writhe, and you can feel the rage rising in you. Rage is frustration, and violence is submission to it. Having been cursed with a violent temper, I hoped that the strict and harsh discipline of a martial art would cure, or at least control it. Temper is not a prideful or dignified thing.

"Hitotsu! Kekki no yu o imashimuru koto!"

The dojo oath, the last of the five parts . . . to guard against impetuous courage, hot temper. As I reached the dojo door I felt ashamed.

In general, boxers, wrestlers, Judoka and Karateka are gentle people, not given to loud talk and overt aggression. I think that Karate is special, though, because it is truly a warrior art, and its development into a sport has only recently begun. In boxing, the match can be stopped, the towel can be thrown into the ring, blows of a certain nature are forbidden, punching below the belt is forbidden. In both wrestling and Judo, the match can be decided by submission, by a fall, by a hold-down. Many moves are forbidden. They too are fighting arts, but they have gone a long way in their evolution toward a sport form. There is no submission in Karate, and if the opponent is thrown, the throw is followed by a kick or a punch, and the theoretical object in a Karate fight would be to kill the opponent.

Karate is evolving toward a sport form, but this development has come only over the past couple of decades. The sport and tournament part of Karate is still only a part, less than half of the art. It is the Western nature to like cups and medals and ribbons and trophies, and it is in the United States where tournament Karate has really caught on. Personally, I dislike tournaments, even though I have taken part in them. Yet tournament Karate is exciting to watch. Rules are evolving. In tournaments, straight finger attacks to the eyes are out. Judges tend to disregard a lot of fast strikes to the head, neck and spine, which are potentially lethal, yet they give points for straight punches to the middle which probably would not down a muscular man. I think that Karate as a sport is very fast developing, and we will end up with weight divisions, rounds, fouls, champions (actually we already have those), heros, and worst of all, spectators . . . armchair Karate men who have never stepped onto a dojo floor. But it hasn't all happened yet.

As things stand now, even those men who are keen on tournaments still practice Karate as an art, know their kata, are adept in "real" fighting.

But for me, and for many like me, Karate is not a sport.

I'm sure we all believed in the fifth tenet of the dojo oath, but stories are still told of fights that this or that Karateka had been involved in.

In a coffee shop one day I was told a story about one of our teachers (whose name I will not disclose). He ranked fourth dan at the time. He had been sipping beer in a bar when a drunk started to trouble him and insist on buying the Karateka a whisky. Politely, the drink was refused, but the drunk was insistent, and belligerently ordered the drink anyway. They argued about it, and the Karateka was firm. He didn't want the drink. Angered, the drunk took the glass and emptied it over the Karateka's suit. He was struck just hard enough to knock him out, and he fell to the floor. The Karateka stood very calmly and apologized, paid for the drinks, and tried to leave. But the drunk had been a gangster, and the bar was full of other members of his society. They tried to prevent the Karate teacher from leaving, and between his seat and the door, thirteen supposedly-hardened street fighters felt the force of his counter attacks and had to be hospitalized.

The story was told to me with great relish, and I enjoyed it.

"What happened then?"

"Oh, well, the police were involved, but they were gangsters you see, and there were so many of them, but . . . sensei was reprimanded. He was lucky that none of them died, but I think he hit them so they would not die. He is very good." The teller's face became serious, and he adopted a righteous attitude. "The association banned him from the dojo for six months. He should not have fought them, because he is a Karate teacher. He felt very ashamed."

I gave him a look which said, oh, sure. The sempai grinned.

"But of course, the other teachers used to practice with him privately, and so did his best students."

I knew that my sempai, the one who told the story. was one of the teacher's "best students."

To present another side of the picture, two young first degree black belts from a university club picked trouble with gangsters and were knifed to death. They were drunk, looking for trouble, and only ranking first dan.

Another case, even uglier, is of a student in Takushoku University who got behind in his grades and tried to withdraw from the Karate club. In defense of my dojo, I will say that this club was not the main club, organized and taught by JKA. Anyway, the student was in such terror of the other members of his club that he tried to avoid going back to school. His father wrote a letter to the dean, explaining the case. Nonetheless, the student was ordered by his Karate sempai to appear for one last practice, and there to explain his lack of "spirit" and his true reasons for wishing to leave the club. At this last session they beat him so badly that he died.

The Karateka that I knew were as disgusted as I was at the incident, but it was not the only one by any means. Karate in the hands of a fanatic, and especially when it becomes the tool of a fanatical, quasi-political group, can be an awful thing.

Karate's brighter side is tranquillity and gentleness, but its satanic side is secrecy and militancy.

The Japanese police, whom I respect more than any other police force except the British, lean very heavily on anyone involved in a brawl. If the offender is a martial artist he is in very hot water indeed. On reaching the first dan grade, the martial artist is registered, and this information is readily available to the police. Misuse of a martial art is considered to be as bad as the use of a weapon.

The Japanese are a fighting nation, but in the four and a half years I have lived in Japan, I saw fewer street and bar fights than I saw in a month in England. A typical Japanese paradox. In a nation with so many dojos, boxing, kick-boxing and wrestling gyms, you can walk with perfect safety, alone, at any time of the day or night, in any Japanese city. Can you say that of any other country? What about the United States? Fiercely brave fighters in war or contest, the Japanese are generally extremely peaceable and well-controlled. I believe that this is the result of the warrior's code, Bushido, which has permeated even the life of a modern Japanese.

Donn Draeger and Nakayama sensei were writing a series of books together. These books, called *Practical*

Karate,* were to give the average guy a series of self-defense responses against various situations. Donn asked me to be one of the thugs, the attackers, and I excitedly agreed.

Looking at him, nobody would guess that Mr. Nakayama is the Chief Instructor of the largest Karate group in Japan. He is a quiet, well-dressed, soft-spoken gentleman. Donn, on the other hand, looks tough. He is big, muscular, and with a craggy face. A truly excellent combination.

We worked out most of the situations in a park quite near the Yotsuya dojo, and a few in our old house in Ichigaya. I got my pictures in volumes three and four, getting slaughtered by Nakayama sensei.

There were five of us foreign "thugs," all much bigger than Nakayama sensei, all students of martial arts, and all dressed in casual clothes. The sensei wore a blazer, smartly-creased trousers, white shirt and tie. For the sake of the photographs, a fine day was chosen, and it was pleasant to be outside. We laughed and joked until the time came to start work.

Donn wanted each situation to be realistic, and between us we pooled our ideas, remembered actual fights, brought up many suggestions to Nakayama sensei, who listened with interest and patience. When time came to attack, we came on strong. The sensei got violently seized by the collar, by the throat, by the crotch. We went for him with clubs, sticks, broken bottles, razors, knives. He handled it all with such precise and focused action that none of us ever got hurt. He hardly ever ruffled his hair or clothes, and yet I knew that the

---

* *Practical Karate*, by M. Nakayama and Donn F. Draeger, published by Charles E. Tuttle, in four volumes. This soft-cover series has been immensely popular and translated into many languages.

difference between living or dying under one of his focused blows lay only in his mind.

We held many sessions, and it was a lot of work, but I learned a great deal about self defense—it was as good as private lessons from the Chief Instructor.

But that was not all that I learned. One day, when we were waiting at the Yotsuya subway station, the train pulled in and a laborer barged out, crashing into Nakayama sensei. The man was a few feet away from me, but I tensed. He cursed the Karate teacher, and had it been I, I would have shown him whom he could and could not shove around. But Nakayama sensei bowed very slightly and apologized, showing not even the slightest annoyance. The man went off, still muttering, and we all stepped onto the train.

And later, I remembered what Sonako had said to me, after a man had insulted her for being with me, and I had gone into a dangerous rage, and had been prevented from attacking him.

"If a dog barks at you," she said, her face troubled, "do you hate the dog? Do you want to kill it? No, it is foolish, let us forget."

Is it in the Celtic genes to nurture a grudge? To foster anger? I discovered that I could exorcise these unpleasant feelings with the makiwara, that by training, fury could pass into coldness, and coldness into nothing at all.

For the time being, that would have to do.

∽ chapter six ∽

Once, Sonako said to me, "No, people like you are not bad. Your heart is wild, but it isn't bad. You are a primitive. However, there is no place for primitives in civilized countries. You must become civilized or you won't survive."

What is a primitive? I think it is a man who is often hungry. He is always looking, always listening, always feeling, always smelling. He is aware and concerned with what is immediately present, and unconcerned with Great Things of National Importance. He is a hunter, though not necessarily of animals. A man can have a full belly and still be hungry for something. It is only when a man has plenty of everything that he becomes really civilized. But the civilized man is dependent on people he has no feeling for, and they depend on him in turn. Hunter, farmer, merchant—that is the order of progression. Very few merchants have time to be concerned with the smell of the earth, or the direction of the wind, with the cry of a bird or beast or the shapes of clouds.

And what of the warrior? Perhaps he is a primitive too. In the natures of primitive and warrior, all opposites are clearly defined. Good and bad. Violent and gentle.

Spring came to Japan, and cherry blossoms scattered their frail beauty in the parks and streets. My savings from the Arctic Expedition were gone. My tourist visa had been renewed four times, thanks to the benevolence of the Japanese government and the personal sponsorship of Takagi sensei. But to live any longer in Japan I had to change my visa. The last extension on my tourist visa had been granted. I would have to leave the country to get the required documents, and it wouldn't be a bad idea to get some money either.

Visas and money were not the only complications in my life. I had decided to marry Sonako, and of course, for somebody like me, not yet twenty-three, marriage was impractical. I had no steady job, and the only kind of work I was any good at was of the wild, adventuring, expeditioning kind. I had blown several thousand dollars and had had a hell of a good time, and although responsible in my own way, I was irresponsible in the eyes of society. Yet Sonako knew and accepted all of this, and when I asked her mother (her father had died in the hands of the Russians at the end of the war) in my stiff and awkward Japanese if I might marry her daughter, permission was granted.

In early June, we were married by signing the proper forms at our local ward office, and a couple of weeks later I bought a return ticket to Canada, and left my new wife to go on an expedition to Great Bear Lake. Unless things happened in Canada, and I decided to bring Sonako over to join me at the end of the expedition, then I would return to Japan in the fall, and we would have a proper wedding in a church.

And so, for the summer of 1963, I was assistant to Dr. Lionel Johnson of the Fisheries Research Board of Canada, working on a survey of Great Bear Lake, which had an area of 11,800 square miles, and during the summer we were to sail every corner of it, charting its depths and contours, netting and examining the fish, sampling the plankton and the creatures and plants of the bottom, analyzing the water.

And thus I was sitting on a rock on the high cliffs of the eastern shores of Great Bear Lake. It was my fifth summer in the Arctic. The lake stretched vast and blue as the sky on which feathers of cirrus were traced. Nothing disturbed the lake, big as a sea. Visibility was good, and for forty miles I could see the hills and cliffs of the McTavish Arm. Distant hills, losing their neighbors in a blue haze.

Below me were the buildings of the Port Radium mine. Many of them were abandoned now. This mine supplied the uranium ore from which the bombs of Hiroshima and Nagasaki were manufactured. Now they mined silver, and the ship which we had chartered, the *Radium Gilbert*, was used to tow the ore on barges across the lake to the mouth of the Bear River, at Fort Franklin.

Often in my life I have perceived strong coincidences which have set me to wondering what significance I should draw from them. Lines of fate, connecting one thing to another. For me, the Canadian north had always been a place of peace, and yet on this particular expedition, immediately after I had made strong ties to Japan, I had come to the origin of the atomic suns that burnt out the military heart of Japan. Of what significance was this?

Japan. Canada. Ravens wheeling and stunting off the cliffs. The old mine below. White buildings with green roofs, clinging to steep, rocky slopes.

The natural harbor of Port Radium lay in the shadow of the hills, but on my vantage point upon the high cliffs, I was still in the gentle warmth of the evening sun. It was the month of August. The expedition was more than half finished, and the decision to return to Japan and continue to follow the Karate way was set in my heart and in my mind; and yet the ghosts of self-doubt intruded from time to time. I was married now. I must be responsible. But to define the terms of responsibility?

The sun's reflection off the lake was painful to the eyes, but the gentle hues of the distant hills—golden, blue, green, purple—were soothing. To set my vision on distant hills helped me to relax my focus, and to think.

On our last trip in the *Radium Gilbert* we came across the lake from Fort Franklin, bringing a passenger to the mine. We had all talked about this and that, and I had talked about Japan.

"What were you doing there? Were you with the military or something?"

"No," I had answered. "I went to Japan to study Judo and Karate."

"What the hell for? What good is it going to do you?"

"Because I want to. I'm going back after this is over."

The man shook his head. "Some people have it easy. Christ. Just go and do what you want. But tell me, this Karate stuff—can you eat it?"

Of course, he meant to ask if Karate was "useful." "Useful." Could you ever explain? Nobody ever asked me that kind of question in Japan. Yet in Canada, so many people had exhibited the same reaction. To many, it seemed ridiculous for a man to devote two years or so to a full-time study of an activity that was not "useful."

·62·

Some people had even reacted with hostility. In harbor, a mine official had come on the boat. The subject was brought up again, and this time not by me.

"Ah!" He made the sound with impatience. "This Karate is no good. A boxer can lick you any day."

"Oh. Are you a boxer?"

"I've done a little bit in the army." When a Westerner says he "has done a little bit" he usually means he has watched it, or done it once. "Karate's a load of baloney."

"I've seen a man put his finger tips through three-inch-thick boards. I've seen a man kick to the side of the head so hard and so fast that he broke four boards. I've seen a man drive his fist through a pile of roofing tiles a foot and a half high. I've seen punches that broke two-by-four timbers, and blows with the edge of the hand that have cracked three housebricks, one on top of the other. I've seen it, and you haven't. You are in no position to judge anything."

"Bullshit. You're full of bullshit."

I became angry, and thought about pounding hell out of him. But then I *saw*. He was over forty, flabby, and with a sizable paunch. He was at an age when he resented his past physical attractiveness, and the present physical excellence of youth. Fat people are usually jolly, but paunchy men tend to be aggressive. This man no doubt tried to kid himself that he was still as good as he used to be. What the hell.

"Think what you want to think," I said, and let it go.

When I remembered things like that, I got angry, but with no good reason. To get rid of this kind of anger, and to purge the ghosts of doubt, I had come up the hill. It was just getting a little chilly now. The sun had almost dipped into the lake, and as its angle changed, the surface of the waters became a brilliant, blinding orange. But directly below me I could still see down through the crystal waters, to the shadowy forms of submerged rocks and the shape of a sunken barge. A solitary gull was hanging in the flame of the setting sun.

Over the mine buildings, I watched the black form of a raven, gliding silently, steering his flight with fan-shaped tail feathers. Here was freedom. But if it was freedom I had been searching for, then I never would have married.

I had just got a letter from Seto Shiunske, my sempai and my friend. In the last few months in Japan he had become my very close friend and confidant, and his family, especially his kind and energetic mother, had taken me under their wing. And now his letter, with its quaint English and its spelling mistakes, brought such a strong nostalgia for Japan that I could hardly bear it. I took it out of my back pocket and read it again.

Dear My brother Nicol,

How are you, What are you doing now? fishing? hunting a bird? or looking to sky to making poetry?

In this day the Tokyo have hot day is still burning, as soon as school is begin, because I am very busy to play and practice Karate and go to beach.

As soon as Autumn come and Bon day already to pass, the jovial pomp and parade was end,

This month 25th we have Economics seminar Summer lodging about one week at Chiba beach house,

My mother want you to come to my house with your wife when you come back to Japan,

Enclosed your letter that was sent to you in care of the Karate office,

Your best looking friend,
Shiunske Seto.

I smiled, and put the letter back in my pocket. The enclosed letter he mentioned was from an old girl friend, now in Australia.

". . . or looking to sky to making poetry?" My friend in Japan could understand me so well, even though his English and my Japanese were not good enough for easy and fluent communication.

Absentmindedly, I picked a wild raspberry. There were thousands of them over this slope. The solitary gull was gliding silently now, and the raven was pecking at garbage. The gull was winding down like a paper airplane. I tried to crystallize what I thought and what I felt, but my thoughts and feelings were in symbols rather than in ordered, logical rationalizations.

I rose from my rock seat and began to pick my way down to the path that led into Port Radium. The ship's lights were on. Someone came out of the galley and tossed slops into the harbor. The gull swooped, down, down, down. It became a white speck on the water. As I descended, the thumping of the ship's generators became more distinct.

Certainly, I would go back to Japan, and follow the Karate way, and live for a while with my wife in the country of her birth.

∿ chapter seven ∿

Mrs. Atsumi, my mother-in-law, had bought a house in Akitsu, a little village just inside the outer boundaries of greater Tokyo. I was so happy when she invited Sonako and me to live in the house with her and to use the six-tatami room upstairs; a bright, airy little place that overlooked fields and woods and a scattering of other small houses.

Akitsu station was thirty-five minutes by fast train from Ikebukuro, a main suburb from which all parts of the city could be reached by train and subway. Unfortunately, it was going to take me three hours a day to commute to the Yotsuya dojo, but that didn't matter; I could read and think and study Japanese on the trains.

From Akitsu station, with its summer swallows' nests, its pigeons, and the goldfish ponds which the station master cherished, I had to walk home through the main street of the village with its friendly, busy little shops, and then past fields and bamboo groves, and under tall elms and cedars, and then across a little bridge until I reached our house. It was a fifteen-minute

walk along a narrow road bordered by carefully cropped tea hedges, past ancient stone Buddha statues—wayside shrines—and big old thatched farm houses with their lines of white oak trees standing guard around them. I could watch the people working in the fields, and see raucous long-tailed jays in the high branches of trees, and also sparrows and shrikes and crows, and even an owl once in a while. Such a relief from downtown Tokyo!

From that summer expedition to Great Bear Lake, I had fallen into a way of life that was truly Japanese, and a hundred-fold more real and joyful than my foreign-bachelor isolation. I was part of a family now. I had a wife, a mother-in-law, sisters, cousins. Each day was an object lesson in living, and I had so much to learn.

Apart from a French Catholic priest who spoke no English, we knew no foreigners in Akitsu. To learn to speak and understand Japanese was very important to me now, and apart from being an official student of the Karate dojo, with a student visa, I was also enrolled in the Tokyo School of the Japanese Language for afternoon classes. In the evenings, to stretch out my all-too-meager savings, I taught English conversation at a couple of English Conversation Schools (of which there are many in Tokyo).

The Japan that I had read and dreamed about began to unfold to me, and even now as I try to write about how I felt, or about what it all meant to me, a thousand images flood my mind, each seeming so precious.

My own personal happiness was reflected from my friends, especially my three sempai, Sasaki, Okuda and Seto. They in particular no longer gave me the leeway or patronization reserved for gauche foreign visitors. They undertook my education in earnest.

Soon after I had returned to the dojo after the summer away, I got my right arm very badly bruised from directly blocking a very powerful kick. The arm was purple, black, puce and green from elbow to wrist. I took the kick on a Wednesday, and on Thursday the dojo was closed for teacher's practice, so I trained at home as usual, strengthening my own kicks with iron clogs. On Friday I went to the dojo and attended the morning class, but when it came time for the "kumite" or "fighting" part of the lesson, I bowed out of the dojo, not wanting to hurt my arm anymore.

Okuda came out of the dojo and berated me for leaving the class. I protested—"But my arm . . ."

"No difference! You have worn your karategi and you have entered the lesson. It is improper and impolite to leave before the end, especially for such a minor affair. Come back in!"

Once back in the dojo I had to fight, and if I had thought that the others would go easy on the injured arm, then I was much mistaken. In favoring the injured arm I showed it to my opponents as a weakness, and as such it was used. The rest of the lesson was a fierce and angered misery of jolting pain and subdued rage. But I surprised myself and fought well, defeating a couple of blue belts.

As we were changing, after the cold shower outside, I asked another black belt why my sempai had disregarded the fact that I had an injury.

"They did not disregard it," he replied. "They did this for your own sake. If you put on your green belt and step onto the dojo floor you signify that you are willing to accept the responsibility of your actions and of your rank. You must therefore be willing to fight, willing to win, willing to lose. I watched you, Nic-san. You fought well. So do not expect us to pamper to your weaknesses. We would be very bad sempai if we did that. Your weakness would only be magnified, and soon any excuse could stop you from fighting—or to fight and not accept the results. We are like soldiers. When a soldier puts on his uniform, carries a weapon and goes to war, he is obviously willing to fight and kill his enemies. If he is willing to kill, then he must be prepared to die. It is only right. We must cultivate spirit. You must be grateful to your sempai for showing you so much attention. If Okuda did not care about you, he would have let you leave. Understand?"

I bowed. "Yes! I understand!"

And so I learned that if ever I had an injury serious enough for me to want to protect it, I either fought hard enough to defend the injury, or I just didn't go to the dojo. You couldn't go and just watch. You got ordered out onto the floor. It was reasoned that if you were fit enough to walk around, catch trains, stand on two feet, then you were fit enough to train. By these means we were to learn "spirit." The dojo was a theater of life and death. No favors were granted for weaknesses, and the degree of pressure put upon you was equal to the color of the belt and to the rank which you bore.

But the color of a belt is not everything. A high-ranking student from another dojo might come to train, and out of courtesy, decline to wear his color. Indeed, once I fought with a white belt and was very soundly beaten. His movements were fast and focused, and his roundhouse kicks whipped at my head too fast for me to block. I felt shame, for a green belt to be beaten by a white belt, I thought, was very poor. The sempai were laughing at me. Later, after much teasing, they told me that the "white belt" had in fact held the rank of first dan black belt.

"Then why does he wear white?" I asked, with some indignation.

"For nearly three years he has not trained at the dojo, and thus he does not feel worthy of the black belt. Later, after he is in good condition, our sensei will tell him to wear his rank again."

The discipline of the dojo was harsh, but conversely, slack or insincere students were not pushed. Another Japanese paradox. Perhaps hard to understand, but for one thing, such a student was always of a lower grade. Without sincerity and hard training you could not win through to the colored belts. A white belt could slack off, and bow out of the dojo without shedding a drop of sweat—that was up to him. He would be ignored. However, bad manners and lack of dojo etiquette were dealt with very severely. Foreigners, however, could be a problem. They had so much to learn that to an extent their ignorance was tolerated until they showed sincerity and the desire to learn.

It was because of this very tolerance that unpleasantness developed. There were two Canadians training at the dojo, nice enough fellows, hard working in their way, but ignorant and boorish to extreme. I could never understand why the hell either of them came to Japan, and I felt embarrassment for my adopted country. They resisted every move to correct their behavior. They laughed and joked and acted in an unseemly manner in the dojo. They walked and lounged around like slovenly louts. They refused to learn the kata, saying that they wanted only to fight. And fight they did, fairly well, but already we could all see that they were soon reaching their plateau, and after that could not progress without development of mind and spirit.

Our sensei should have leaned hard on them, and forced them, physically if need be, to conform. They had the authority and strength to do so. But the sensei let things slide because the two men were strangers, and as such were expected to behave like badly-brought-up children. And like spoiled children, the two Canadians got worse and worse.

The most intolerable thing about them though was the fact that they were not very clean. I don't know how often they bathed, but certainly neither of them ever washed their karategi. Soon everybody complained of the stink. The majority of Japanese believe that foreigners, Westerners in particular, are a stinky bunch, and these two were the epitome, the perfect example, to reinforce an old prejudice. The Japanese are a scrupulously clean people, and for them it was especially distressing. The stench was overpowering. Angered students time and time again tossed the offending uniforms out of a window. Even Donn Draeger got to hear about it and had words with them, to no avail.

It is sadly true that there is a stereotyped image of toughness in North America—it goes with coarse speech and rough manners, with swagger and disregard for traditions and social niceties. It is an unfortunate image, enhanced by American movies of a decade or so past, and quite false, for the truly tough North American is not like that at all.

Anyway, one day I was so nauseated by the stink of the two Canadians that I left the dojo, and when Enoeda sensei told me to go back in, I refused.

He was quite taken aback, because nobody refused him. "What!"

"I am sorry, sensei, I refuse to go back in."

"Why?"

"The dojo is a place to respect, but our dojo stinks. I will not train in there because I will vomit. Forgive me."

In defense of my actions I must state that I am not a finicky or delicate individual. Even at that time I had lived under primitive conditions, performed autopsies on long-dead seals, eaten raw and slightly rotten meat with Eskimo, and gone unwashed for periods of time. But this was worse by far.

Enoeda sensei glowered and nodded, letting me go. As soon as the two Canadians came out of the dojo he grabbed them both. Neither of them spoke much Japanese.

"You smell bad. Wash. You not go into dojo again and make bad smell. Wash!"

As soon as he turned away the Canadians grinned at each other. See? These Japs just couldn't take it.

Within a few weeks the situation grew very tense. Okuda was in a fury. He had watched it all develop and said that if a teacher didn't fix the Canadians, then he or somebody else would. I later heard other threats, and they increased in violence and vehemence. The Canadians were on the books to get a beating, and I knew they would try to fight, and get so much worse for it.

On thinking of the struggle I had been fighting within myself to control my own temper through the discipline of Karate, I felt a disappointment. And so I prepared a little speech, having learned all the right words, and thus prepared I confronted Takagi sensei. He was at his desk. He looked up at me. The office was muggy with the steam from the tea kettle on the kerosene stove. Two other teachers were standing by, one in his karategi.

"Takagi sensei, I am thinking about withdrawing from this school." Surprise came into his eyes. It was he who had sponsored me, got me through the first eight months of difficulties with the Immigration Authorities. The other teachers looked up.

"Two foreigners at this dojo have shown bad manners and have behaved without etiquette. In my thoughts, this is not only their fault, but the fault of the teachers for not being strict with them as they would with a Japanese. I have believed in the principles of equality. Now these foreigners have angered some people to such an extent that I have heard several threats. They are mere white belts, but they are being threatened by second and third dan Karateka. This is against the morals of the dojo. If these men are harmed I would not be able to respect the dojo." I bowed as I finished my speech.

Takagi sensei stood up and bowed to me. "Thank you, Mr. Nicol, for bringing this matter so clearly to my attention. I knew of the trouble, but not of the threats. Do not worry. I will handle it."

I bowed again and went in to practice. I could hear short and angry questions being asked.

The next week, for the first time in the history of the Japan Karate Association in Tokyo, two foreign students were handed notice of expulsion. It was done with cold ceremony. They had received one last warning, but it had not worked.

Later, they laughed about it, but I think it shocked them a little. They don't know how lucky they were. As some of the black belts had said, they might have had "their parts scattered."

I write this now ten years later, and I am now in the position of having to stand before a class and teach

Karate, and well I remember how hard it was to correct bad manners after they have been ignored. If any student in our class steps across the line, he gets hell, and if he objects, he is asked to leave. If he refuses to leave, he is bodily removed. I am a Westerner myself, and recognize that often in the Western nations gentleness and politeness can be misunderstood as weakness. We are polite and gentle—up to a point. Would that I had the strength of a true master, like Mr. Nakayama and a few others, who can be gentle always!

Two weeks later. While free fighting with a brown belt I dropped my arm to stop a powerful side thrust kick (delivered with the edge of the foot in a sideways thrust from the hip). The arm took the force of the kick and I was hurled against the wooden wall. The word was out now, and foreigners no longer got special favors, so we were all going through the mill. I fought hard, and it was not until that night, hanging from a strap ring in the crowded Akitsu train, trying to read between the jostling rushes that punctuated each station stop, that the arm injured before and now anew began to ache. Like a bastard.

The following morning it had stiffened up, but I went to the dojo, where my sempai, especially Okuda-san, were solicitous about it, and helped me bind it up with an elastic bandage. Was I sure that I should practice? Oh yes, I was sure.

The first part of the lesson was very basic, mostly repeated lunge punches and front snapping kicks, but performed with great intensity, and with each move we had to drive our bodies forward, hips low and full of power, moving ten or twelve feet across the floor with each lunge, sweat-soaked karategi slapping with the focus, and the dojo filling with the thunder of our shouts, and drops of sweat marking myriad spots on the dark floor.

Then there was a two-minute break before the black belts lined up to face the rest of us. They stood relaxed, feet apart, a few of them with their black belts already fulfilling the circle—returning to whiteness by the fraying of constant use. We lower graders presented ourselves in line to them, and at a command from the teacher, the front man in each line fought a black belt until he was defeated. It was a great test for the black belts, for most of the colored belts attacked furiously, knowing that they would be defeated, but at the same time wishing to make a good fight of it. We had strength, but poor control, so the black belt had to be doubly aware of our blows. For the most part, the furious onslaughts were parried almost contemptuously until a final "killing blow" was driven home.

Our line faced Okuda. A tall Japanese student, rather awkward despite his green belt, waited his turn to fight in front of me. He bowed and stepped out, his nervousness clearly visible in his eyes and movements. Perhaps the barrage of sound and the fierce fighting going on around him had awed him. He hung back.

Okuda feinted a lunge, and the fellow jumped back like a scared kitten. "Fight!" Okuda glared and yelled at him, but still the student minced around, tossing out half-hearted kicks, taking care to keep his distance. "Is this Karate? Fight!" Now all those not actually fighting were looking at the two of them. It was inevitable. By not fighting, the student betrayed his rank, his teachers, his dojo. By not fighting he insulted his sempai, from whom he should have had nothing to fear, for his blows were under control. Okuda leaped forward, and with one hand he seized the student by the throat and drove him out of an open window. The window was quite high off the dojo floor, so to do this, the student's body had to leave the ground, his feet clearing the floor by two feet or more. The force of the lunge took him through the window and landed him in the muck outside. Tokyo is a smoggy place. In hard training, students often brought up muck from their lungs, and they often sneaked over to that particular window to spit outside on a pile of rubble and dirt. He was gone from sight. Nobody dared to look, but we knew he had to be covered with crap. The teacher sauntered over to the window and peered out.

"Have you received injury?"

"No."

"Then come back in!"

The student started to come through the window, but gently, the teacher pushed him back with one hand on his chest.

"Oh no. It is ill-mannered to leave and enter by a window. We will excuse the exit, but use the front door now. And wash your feet when you come in."

The poor guy had to walk around via a busy street, receiving many stares. After today, I knew he would either quit the dojo, or would begin to fight like a tiger.

And thus my turn came, and I was facing Okuda, whose eyes were fierce, and whose chest was runneled with sweat. With fury, and with all the strength and speed I could muster, I attacked him. He deflected the attack and hurled me to the floor with a footsweep, following with a thrusting heel to my ribs. I fell onto the bad arm and it hurt, but I rolled over and came immediately to my feet, attacking him again. This time he did not throw me, but let me spar with him, slowing down his movements so that I could see and understand the openings. At the end of it he told me that it was well done, then yelled out "Next!" with a ferocity that might have scared a lion.

I went to the back of the line, as I should have, but the teacher grabbed me and put me in front of another fierce-eyed black belt, and in the eyes of the teacher I thought I saw the suspicion of a grin.

By the end of it all my right arm hung like a limp rag, and after the shower I had to get another student to help me into my jacket.

As I went to leave, Takagi sensei stopped me.

"Nicol. You have hurt your arm. Let me see."

With difficulty, I got the jacket off and rolled up the sleeve. He poked at it.

"Ah, this is just a bruise on the muscle, that is nothing. Move your arm this way."

I tried, and pains knifed through the elbow.

"Hmm. There is no fracture. I don't think that bandage you wore would help much. Give me the arm. Here, sit down."

With his thumbs, he found the sore point and pressed very firmly. The pain was exquisite, and almost pleasurable in its intensity, and gradually, as he pressed, the pain faded away. He found another point and pressed that with both thumbs, and I felt the same sharp pain, fading as he pressed.

"Now move your arm like this."

I did so, and to my astonishment, the pain was all gone, and the joint moved freely. I thanked him and asked him why he had known this.

"Our knowledge of the body does not only give us the power to inflict injury and death; it also gives us knowledge to relieve pain and to retrieve from death. Maybe you will one day learn enough to understand.

Now, tonight, take a hot, hot bath, take a drink of plum wine, and come back tomorrow to train hard. Soon you must take the examination for blue belt."

I left the dojo, greatly elevated in spirit, and much at peace with myself.

∽ chapter eight ∽

Mr. Hirokazu Kanazawa, sixth dan, had returned to Tokyo after teaching a couple of years in Hawaii. Two times All Japan champion, having won it once with a broken arm, Kanazawa sensei was famous for his incredible speed and superb style. He was quite tall, and slim, but each muscle in his body had the definition of an anatomical chart. He was very popular, got along with everybody, always had a smile and words of encouragement.

The first time I met him, he and Takagi sensei were talking, and as I bowed to them and went to go into the changing room, Takagi sensei called me over.

"This is Nicol. He can speak Japanese."

I bowed. "It is the first time we meet, sensei."

We exchanged polite greetings and Kanazawa sensei smiled. "Nicol. What did you first learn at the dojo?"

The question surprised me, but I answered. "I learned 'kihon' [basic movements]."

"Yes. Who brought Karate to Japan?"

"Karate was brought to Japan by the Master Funakoshi."

The two teachers exchanged glances.

"Good. Next week you will appear on NHK [the national television] with Kanazawa sensei. They will ask you many questions and you will answer in Japanese. You have learned well. Your wife is a good teacher."

For the week before this TV appearance, Kanazawa sensei coached me in the classical one-point attack and counterattack—in which both the attacker and the receiver know the target and style of the attack to be delivered. The two opponents bow, and while one remains in the "shizentai" or natural position—feet apart, hands in fists in front of him—the other adopts a "kamae"—a fighting position in the front forward stance. The attacker tells the receiver what he will do, and then he attacks, using only one technique, but with much power. The receiver must block or avoid the attack, then counter strongly, also with one movement, giving a shout, or "kiai," as he does so. Then they both move back into the formal "ready" position. With this technique the Karateka learns distance, timing and control. He learns to attack strongly, and to defend strongly and cleanly. It is only after countless thousands of repetitions of such attack and defense movements that he can go on to "jiyu kumite"—a free exchange of attack and counterattack.

Kanazawa sensei also coached me in the fourth Heian kata, the prerequisite of the fifth kyu, or blue belt (sometimes called "purple"). It is a very beautiful kata, with full movements, with elbow strikes, knife hand and back fist strikes, with front kicks, side kicks and blows with the knee, with intricate steps and difficult pivotings and shiftings of balance. It is a favorite kata for group demonstrations.

Kanazawa sensei was stern, but in a very different way from the others, for his easy friendliness came out even during practice. I admired all of the teachers, but he was the one whose style I would most like to emulate. Long and lithe of movement, and to me, more graceful, beautiful, and certainly more masculine, than the greatest of ballet dancers.

We worked hard, but as I suspected, the TV show was a pretty corny deal. They just wanted a foreigner who could do a little Karate and who could understand a little Japanese. The Japanese seem to get a kick out of hearing foreigners trying to speak their language. It was a panel game, and three foreigners, me and two non-Karateka, got dressed up in our karategi and green belts and faced a panel of four famous television personalities. They were supposed to guess which of us was the real C. W. Nicol—the foreigner who had come to Japan to learn Karate and "polish his heart." It was a very popular show, occupying prime time, called "This is I." I was supposed to answer truthfully, while the others could lie. At the end, only one of them guessed correctly. Then Kanazawa sensei, a brown belt (an American who could not speak Japanese; otherwise he would have been put on the stand) and I put on a simple demonstration.

After it was all over, and I clutched my little envelope with a small "present," Kanazawa took us all out to a restaurant that specialized in "chanco nabe," a dish highly favored by the Sumo wrestlers, made from fish, vegetables and chicken, cooked on charcoal right in front of us as we sat in a little sort of box of tatami mats such as the patrons of sumo reserve to watch the matches.

We ate, and drank beer and sake until bloated, while Kanazawa sensei regaled us with tales of his Hawaiian stay, making us hoot with laughter, partly by his animated manner of storytelling, and partly by his forceful mixture of Japanese and English. Like the first night he spent in a Western hotel, when he had left his room to go to the bathroom, dressed only in a towel, then locked himself out of his room, ran around in the corridor half-naked, trying to get people to understand his predicament . . .

And like the time a huge, hulking he-man wrestler had come to challenge him at the Karate school. ". . . So he hold out his hand you see, to shake hands, so I shake hands with him, but he is very strong, and he squeeze, very, very hard. I hold my hand like this . . . Oh! Very hurt! You are so strong! And this wrestler say that Karate is no good, and he wants to fight me. He is very foolish, and I don't care, but he brings lots of people with him to see, and for the newspapers, so I say, OK, we will fight, but first you fetch your lawyer and I fetch a lawyer, and together we write a paper; if you kill me, it is not your fault, and if I kill you, it is not my fault, and then we sign the paper and we fight, but I think maybe you are going to die."

Then with a one-knuckle fist, he delivered a staccato blow to the ribs, and the man, more than twice the weight of Kanazawa sensei, doubled over in agony. The sensei then warned him that if he fought, he could rip out his heart, literally rip it out of his chest. And later, I saw proof that he could do it, for he could drive his finger tips like four rifle bullets through four inches of pine boards.

. . . And another time, in a restaurant, a loud-mouth challenged him. "Fine," he said, "but before we fight, I must first warm up." With that he did a sequence of six or seven blindingly fast moves in the empty air, shook his shoulders and smiled at the challenger. "Shall we fight? All warmed up now!" The loud-mouth went back to his seat.

Kanazawa sensei was so fast that he was able to stand twenty feet away from me and warn me to be ready to accept an attack to the jaw. I would stand ready to block. Never was I able to move fast enough to block that punch! Free sparring with him, he could be standing in front of me, leap over my head, lash out with a kick to the back of my neck and be on the ground, behind me, before I could turn around. His demonstrations of breaking were awesome. He would group four people around him, each holding three or four inch-thick pine boards. In less than three seconds he would execute four perfect movements, probably a thrust kick, an elbow strike, a reverse punch and a knifehand blow, and smash all four targets with movements as precise as a kata sequence.

But that was not the most impressive. For there have always been stories of Karate, Kempo and Kung-fu masters who could deliver a blow to the body of an opponent, who would feel pain, but would suffer no surface wounding or bruising on his body, but who would later die of massive internal hemorrhage.

One day, after Kanazawa sensei had smashed a pile of three old red bricks taken from a crumbling wall, he did something which seems physically impossible. The feat of breaking the three bricks, placed flat as they were on a concrete floor, was incredible enough. Most men could not have done it with a hammer, but they broke with a "whump!" as he brought down the edge of his hand on them. But that, he said, was nothing. Another pile of three old bricks was placed. He determined to put his spirit, or "ki," into the middle brick. With a shout, he struck the top of the pile of three bricks, and at times we must accept the incredible, for it was the middle brick, and only the middle brick, that cracked through the middle. There was no trick, and only an audience of a few students.

To explain it? Fist filled the space in time already occupied by the mind, and to facilitate this, the Karateka had to empty his mind in a combat situation. If mind was strong, the blow was strong. It was claimed that mind-force could project itself further and deeper than the actual physical presence of the fist, and could of itself alone alter the state of matter. In perfection, the mind-force, the "ki," of a true master would surround him so that his physical self was inviolate, and he could stop an attacker in his tracks with his "kiai" or shout, or hold him still with his gaze like a stoat with a rabbit.

Anyway, for all his strength and perfection in his art, Kanazawa sensei was easy to be with, witty, amusing, considerate. It was a tremendous evening, and the start of something very special for me. On the way back, in a taxi, he asked me if I had come to Japan to work. I answered that I had come to learn martial arts, especially Karate. He seemed surprised and pleased.

"Well then, soon you must get your brown belt. Be at the dojo at nine-thirty tomorrow, and I will show you how to do the kata properly."

"But sensei, I am still only green belt."

"Yes, but next month you will take an examination for fifth kyu. Train very hard. I will watch you. You must perfect the kata. That is the most important thing."

"You do me honor, sensei."

"You come from your country to learn. It is my obligation to help you."

‿ chapter nine ‿

In savagery and in gentleness, in kindness and in cruelty, and in a seemingly infinite stream of opposites that were not opposites, my teachers, sempai and friends demonstrated the timeless Now, and the essence of the Karate spirit, embodied in the very character of "Kara," which means "emptiness"; and yet still I struggled for understanding just as I struggled with the Japanese language and with the movements and reflexes of the art I practiced. Japan was still an enigma to me, but day by day the pieces fitted, albeit with difficulty, for this was a puzzle of at least four dimensions.

Life as a young husband in a Japanese family was a many-faceted jewel. It was as if Japan teased, and then praised me, and thereby, through her mysteries, set deep roots into my heart.

At first neighbors and others persisted in using my wife's Japanese family name, her maiden name, and would never call her "Nicol," which was her married name. I felt anger and annoyance and imagined all sorts of hidden insults in this, but then that faded into a kind of pride when they started to call me, the foreign husband, by Sonako's Japanese name. Why? Perhaps I had fitted into the order of things. Certainly I was greeted like any other man around the village, and when community groups went out with shovels and rakes to fix the road, I was called on to do my bit. I felt at home, but home was all new and exciting as well as being old and comfortable.

Whenever my schedule permitted, I liked to go shopping with Sonako in the afternoon, to walk along the narrow lanes and paths that were bordered by lines of dense, dark green tea bushes, so fragrant, and in the spring, delicately filigreed with white flowers and new pale emeralds of fresh tea. We would walk past fields as neatly kept as the tidiest of backyard vegetable plots, where country women in baggy smocks weeded and hoed between rows of sweet potatoes, onions, long white radishes and a dozen other types of plants. We called out greetings to them and exchanged comments about the weather.

The change of seasons was marked by the activities of the farmers, and now it was autumn, and the men were spreading leaves, carefully gathered from around the houses and in the woods, raking them into long compost trenches between the rows of vegetables. With such care the soil was fine and rich, and highly productive despite the relatively small area.

In the tall trees that stood sentinel around the mighty thatched roofs of old farmhouses, wind plucked capriciously at leaves and shook the perches of the long-tailed jays. Outside one house, by the step, seven brightly colored umbrellas. In a bamboo grove, an old man with an axe—smack, smack, smack—and I thought of the folk story of the old man who found fairy gold in just such a tall bamboo, and who later found and raised a fairy princess who flew to the moon.

As Sonako and I neared the main village street, the Tokyo rush-hour trains were roaring in like dragons, one every few minutes, disgorging loads of students in tunics, pretty young office girls, dark-suited, white-shirt-and-tie business men ("salary men" to the Japanese), returning shoppers—all now hurrying home as purposefully as they had hurried to work. Massed humanity channeling down the main village street, then dispersing and becoming individuals once more, hurrying along lanes and down paths.

In Akitsu, at least, we got no strange or hostile stares. We were known. I waited and watched as Sonako carefully chose the vegetables for the evening meal (most Japanese wives prefer to shop daily, thus ensuring the freshest of foodstuffs), picking the freshest, firmest and greenest from the open stalls of the greengrocer. From across the street the butcher called out to me. He had some fine beef, saved especially, he said, for me. Each shop was busy with a cluster of housewives and daughters, the older ladies in their kimonos, the front and sleeves protected with a white tie-on smock, and their clogs clattering on the pavement. And from tiny little shops with sliding doors and hanging curtains, tempting smells of chicken and liver "yakitori," dipped in sauce and barbecued on slivers of bamboo over carefully fanned charcoal, the fragrance mixed with the scent of warming sake, tempting many a returning husband to delay his homecoming for an hour or so.

On our way back from shopping, Sonako and I stopped at the rice grinder's shop to place an order. We were invited into the house at the back for green tea and sweet bean paste cakes, and there we talked about many things, about autumn, and the rain, and about thatched roofs and paper umbrellas. I asked about the history of some of the fine old farm houses; Akitsu was so lucky, I remarked, to have escaped the devastating fire-bomb raids of the last war.

The war. It was a subject that figured in many conversations. My father and my uncles had fought in it. Sonako's father had died of starvation in Russian hands, and her uncles had spent their lives and left their bones in jungles here and there in the Pacific and Asia. On both sides of nations ostensibly at peace, wartime propaganda still persisted, tainting opinions and obscuring truth. How often had I read or heard of how cruel and savage the Japanese were, and indeed, only recently I had been reading a book called *The Knights of Bushido*, very popular and in paperback form, written by Lord Russell of Liverpool, describing and decrying the Japanese atrocities—to quote—"lest we should forget."

And of course, as any Britisher or American, or even Australian will sanctimoniously tell you, our side never did anything like that . . .

"Ah," said the rice man, "but we had a big explosion here when a B29 crashed with all its bombs. It blew a big hole in the ground and damaged two houses. You can see the hole, it is still there, on your way back home, just to the left by the crossroad shrine."

Curious about the hole, Sonako and I turned left just before our lane and went via a well-trodden path between tall trees. It was cool and shady there, and a slight drizzle carried the scents of smoke and damp earth. Sure enough, the hole was there, huge and deep, filled now with water and fringed by the delicate green of water plants. A farmer passed by and I asked him what had happened to the wreckage of the plane.

"Oh, it was taken for the war. The government needed the metal." He smiled. "The Americans were bombing Tokyo every day then, and at night we could see the light from the fires."

And the crew?

"They all died. Come this way." He led us on a little, and to our surprise we came upon a beautiful little garden, screened from the road by trees. It was well-kept, with no weeds among the flowers and shrubs, and in the center was a large stone, by which were offerings of food, of sake, and some freshly burnt incense.

"One of us comes here every day, usually Grandmother. They all died in the explosion and our house and that house over there were damaged by the blast. We found them"—he made a face—"and we made their grave there." He shrugged his shoulders and added, almost apologetically, "It was the best we could do."

I looked around at this simple little garden, sitting now on land which was immensely valuable to the land-hungry speculators of greater Tokyo. I nodded, and mumbled thanks, for I did not know what to say.

"What does the character on the stone mean?" I asked my wife.

"Peace," she answered. "They did not know the names of the Americans who died. You know, they did this before the war had finished; the Americans were still our enemies then."

Outside, in the yard of a nearby farmhouse, a little gray-haired old lady bent over a broom, busily sweeping the fallen leaves of a gnarled and ancient persimmon tree. Dark clouds scudded by, over the curves of the eaves. And then came a gust of wind, and a thousand leaves clung to the wet roof, and tears came to my eyes, and my scalp tightened, and the wet leaves and the roof suddenly brought an understanding to me of something that was pure Zen, and therefore wordless, and Sonako and I went home together for supper.

The second Christmas which I spent in Japan should have been a happy one, but it was not. After a quiet day at home we lost by miscarriage what would have been our first child. Late in the night I had to run to the station to try to find a taxi, and when I found one, I had to bargain with the driver, and offer him double his normal fare to take us downtown to the hospital. Christmas Eve was a big time for the taxi drivers to make money from the partygoers returning from bars. Just as I was pleading with the driver, a drunk man tried to push me out of the way, shouting to the driver and waving a note of large denomination. I spun and punched him in the chest. This was the first time I had ever hit anybody since that little skirmish with the May Day demonstrators. The punch was fast, low, from the hips, with feet and ankles well braced on the gravelly road, and I swear the man actually left the ground and landed six feet away from me. He didn't get up, and I got the taxi.

Why tell that? Well, with the awareness that Karate was bringing to me, I was also gaining physical power and speed, even though I was fifteen pounds lighter and two inches less around the biceps than I had been when I first came to Japan. I don't think that blow was greatly spurred by the effects of adrenalin in my system either; although of course I was under stress. No. In a split second I decided to strike the man, rather than waste time pushing and arguing, but I did not want to hit him in the face or the gut, for I guessed it would cause serious injury. Therefore I hit him in the chest. I simply performed a good Karate reverse punch. I did not know the power or the effect it would have on

my "opponent." Of course, I had been told that a Karate punch to the chest, delivered by a master, could actually kill a man, even through body armor, but I was not a master. And so, is Karate not dangerous? So many times this point has been raised and asked of me—does not training in Karate bring great danger, just because of the very deadly power which a truly skilled, and I must stress skilled, Karateka would have? Well, yes, Karate is dangerous. I think that the most dangerous time for most Karateka is when they have reached the brown belt level. At this grade, they are strong and fast, and notoriously rough in free fighting. They are accurate with their blows, and deliver them with power, certainly enough to maim or kill. They have learned to focus, and they have begun to learn fighting spirit. All of this they have learned, but they usually have not learned calmness and tolerance and the state of empty-mind that is brought about by further intensive practice. Moreover, few of them have any idea of the actual effect (or lack of effect!) their blows can have on a human body, and most brown belts, would, in the backs of their minds, like to try out their Karate in a real fight.

But in the last instance, the danger or lack of it stems from the heart and nature of the individual. With the acquisition of fighting skills, a potentially violent man becomes potentially more dangerous; but at the same time, the actual process of training gives release to his violence. Eventually the discipline and release of the fighting art will bring him through the full circle to true gentleness, not merely the repression and false control of his violent nature.

I had been in many street fights, and I had fought as a wrestler in a carnival, but for the first time in my life I had struck with no anger. I struck because I believed, decided, that it was the best thing to do. Was this not one step up?

Some men are truly gentle to begin with, and yet still they turn to a martial art. I was to meet and to become a lifelong friend with such a man.

One evening, returning home with my briefcase slung over my shoulder by the belt of my rolled and tied karategi, I became aware of somebody increasing his pace to walk beside me. "Shit!" I thought to myself, "here's some student wanting to practice his English on me and get a free lesson on the way home." Already I had taught four hours of English conversation that night, and I was in no mood for more. But I had misjudged. The young man spoke to me in Japanese.

"Excuse me, but are you Mr. Nicol?"

"Yes, that is right." I glanced in surprise at him, wondering how he should know me.

"I am Ikeda. Are you interested in martial arts?"

"Indeed. As you see, I have been at the dojo today. Karate."

"Good. Do you have any interest in Kendo?"

"Of course yes, but I have no time to practice."

"I need somebody to train with me. We live quite close. How about Sunday mornings? I think you would enjoy Kendo. Please won't you try it?"

On the way home he explained to me how I should get to his house, and I agreed to come out the next weekend. His straightforward and friendly approach was refreshing, and I looked forward to it.

The following Sunday I left our house earlier than he had specified, and rode Sonako's bicycle along the dusty side roads. Ikeda-san lived down a lane, past fields and a chicken farm. It was a very old part of the village. I left the bike near a fence, and walked the last twenty yards down a very narrow trail through a bamboo grove. The trail opened out onto a farmyard, fronted by a huge, four-hundred-year-old house with a high, sweeping, thatched roof. Trees and bamboo all around. Pillars on the house of two-foot-thick cedar and oak. And on the bare ground in front of the ancient house, Ikeda was performing a solitary ritual of sword drawing, beautiful kata of the art called "Iaido." It was as if that narrow trail through the bamboo had carried me out of the twentieth century and into the feudal period. Ikeda was dressed in kimono and hakama, the dress of the samurai, and in his hands the sword was a thing alive, a pattern of silver light against the somber colors of old wood and brown earth. Did the man move the sword? Or did the sword move the man? As he pirouetted and wheeled, the sword sang around him, and I watched in silence, savoring the rightness of it all—the man and the sword, the house and the nodding, swaying bamboo, sparrows on the thatch undisturbed by human battle ritual. Ikeda stopped like a stone, and for a moment in time the swordsman was utterly motionless; then, with the softest "snick," he returned the sword to its scabbard. Finally he became aware of me, standing at the head of the path, and he bowed and smiled.

"Ah, Nicol-san, you are early. Come, let us go into my house and have tea."

A sculptor in metal, and therefore useful with his hands, Ikeda had built a house and studio for himself on the last remnant of his family land. Sadly, the great old house and the rest of the land had been forfeited by an uncle who had got himself badly into debt. Ikeda led me into his studio, which was cluttered with bronze figures, some finished, some still being worked on, and with the various paraphernalia of his art—oxyacetylene torch, a rack of large gas cylinders, tools, molds. From the ceiling several metal mobiles were suspended, humorous things, poking fun at human instability, or as Ikeda put it "stability within instability." On the walls were drawings, paintings, a large painted kite, shelves of tools, pottery, and various other interesting things, and, of course, a rack of wooden practice swords and bamboo "shinai" (the simulated weapons used for fencing contests). On one wall hung a very old seven-foot-long spear. A pair of cats lorded it over the place, warmed now with a charcoal fire in the brick fireplace in the studio.

The living quarters were separated from the studio by old wooden screens taken from the farmhouse. His wife, Hiroko, came out to be introduced and then bustled around in the kitchen making tea.

Ikeda was a man without fanciful embellishments. He was as direct and strong in his manner as the muscular arms and shoulders he bore as testimony to the effort he put into both sculpture and Kendo. He did not befriend me just because I was a foreigner, and therefore new and strange (and useful for practicing English). Actually, he showed no interest in the English language as such, though he did ask many questions about British and European history. While we sipped our tea in front of the glowing coals, we talked about swords, spears, maces and halberds, about the power of the English longbow to penetrate armor, and about the ways our two cultures had evolved differing philosophies of battle. Ikeda befriended me because he thought I might like to practice the art of the sword.

It is romantic perhaps, but I believe there is something stronger than mere circumstance and coincidence in the forming of long-lasting and deep friendship. I feel that our life-paths can be drawn together, perhaps in order to fulfill some distant and common goal. Thus are strong bonds between people formed. Ten years after our first meeting, Munehiro Ikeda remains one of my closest friends; and as I predicted then, he is now becoming very famous in Japan for his sculptures.

Although he said that grade mattered little to him, and he had not taken an examination for a long time, he ranked around fifth dan in Kendo. His brother was a high-ranking Karateka of the Goju style, and Ikeda had learned a lot from him, and also he was very interested in the old unarmed fighting arts of the samurai —Jujitsu and Yawara. He treasured and duplicated old manuscripts on the subjects, spending hours with scrolls, ink, brushes.

We finished our tea and went outside to begin my first lesson in sword, using heavy oaken practice swords called "boken." Practice swords in Kendo are basically of two types. The boken is close to the weight and feel of the real thing, and is used to practice cutting and parrying, but is never used actually to strike an opponent. In the old days they used to practice fights with the boken and many, many men were killed. In the Meiji period, when even people not of the aristocratic samurai class could learn sword arts, a very light, straight "shinai" was developed, as was fencing armor—mask, gauntlets, breastplate. The shinai is made of split bamboo, and is used to strike a fencing partner, dressed in his armor of course, with full force. The Kendo kata is performed either with real swords or with boken. Two people take part, attacker and receiver, and the blows with the sword are focused just short of actual contact, as with Karate.

Even in that first lesson I saw how much the sword had influenced the techniques and attitude of the Karate fighter. There was the same awareness of distance and territory, the same calm acceptance of battle.

That first day, Ikeda showed me how to hold the sword, how to raise it above my head and strike down for the opponent's head. As in Karate, the weapon did not carry on through the target, but was stopped, as the mind focused on the target and the swordsman's strength was transmitted from hips and lower abdomen through the arms and wrists to the cutting edge of the sword. He showed me, too, how the point of the sword should "cover" the enemy, and how the edge was "alive" in certain positions, and ineffectual or "peaceful" in others. I saw then what one of our Karate teachers had tried to explain to me about the way I held my fists in free fighting—that sometimes I let my fists "die," and thus showed my opponent that my concentration was waning.

Of course, in one day I could accomplish very little skill in the use of the sword, but I had become excited. I saw now what Donn Draeger had said all along—that an unarmed fighter could not be truly rounded in his art until he had learned skill in at least one (non-missile) weapon. When I left Ikeda's house that day I looked forward eagerly to our next session, which was scheduled for the following Sunday morning. A day later, my forearms were aching as they had never ached before. The heavy boken was a superb tool for strengthening the arms and increasing the effectiveness of knife hand blocks and attacks. I got hold of one and started to use it regularly.

Partly through the urging of our friend Donn Draeger, and partly for her own interest and health, Sonako had started lessons in stick fighting at the Tomisaka police dojo, quite near the Kodokan. She went twice a week to study under the Master Shimizu, the greatest teacher and highest rank in Jojitsu. Jojitsu is an ancient art, founded by a warrior priest of the Kuroda clan named Muso Gonnoske. This man had once fought Miyamoto Musashi, Japan's greatest swordsman. All other men who fought Miyamoto were killed or crippled, but Muso fought him to a draw. It is said that the techniques of stick fighting came to him in a dream after long, long contemplation on how to overcome the seemingly invincible two-sworded style of the legendary Miyamoto.

The stick, or "jo," of itself is not an impressive thing to look at. It is only forty-eight inches long and just under one inch in diameter; but in the hands of a skilled person it is an incredible and deadly weapon. Made of seasoned white oak, the ends of it can be driven through ribs or through a braincase like a bullet. A properly delivered blow can actually break a poorer quality sword, such as those mass-produced for the Japanese army in the last war. Donn Draeger described such a breaking at the riot police school. A swordsman faced a stick fighter, who spun his stick around in a great whistling arc to catch the sword on its side. The sword snapped in two. He also told me how they had tried to cut through a "jo" by placing it between two chairs and then cutting down with a two-handed swipe of a sword. The sticks, when reasonably new, are resilient enough to absorb the force of the steel. They bow and spring, not break. The "jo" is a favorite weapon of Japan's ultra-tough riot police, for good reason.

However, the art was developed primarily for travelers such as priests who did not carry other weapons, only the innocent staff that helped them on their way. Apart from the "kihon" or basic exercises, practice of the art consisted of kata against a swordsman. In the formal art of Jojitsu (not to be confused with Jujitsu, which is an unarmed fighting art) there are no kata against unarmed men. To watch, it is ritualistic and graceful, quite suited to the movements of a woman.

When Sonako took it up, I was delighted, for now we could practice something together. I could learn the swordsman's part of the kata (the stick fighter had to learn both) and could let her go through the various kata of defense against the sword. We started to do this on an empty lot in front of our house in Akitsu. Sonako began to get pretty good.

My obvious interest in the warrior arts led me to yet another friendship with our next-door neighbor. He was a fletcher, and made arrows to sell to both the traditional Kyudo (Japanese archery) dojos, as well as to the sport shops that dealt with the Western variety of archery. He held high rank in Kyudo, and we often talked about the Zen that is so inherent in the Japanese art.

It was as if the surface were calmer now, and I could begin to see beneath it, coming face to face with more and more examples of the warrior philosophies of Japan, so often presumed dead or defunct by the West, and so often abused and misunderstood by both Westerners and many young Japanese. I knew now that I had not come to Japan on a wild goose chase. It was all here.

. . . Yes, it was here . . . in the stone of peace by the crater of the crashed plane, in the straight gaze and honesty of the swordsman sculptor, in the serene philosophies of a quiet gentleman making arrows, and in the earnest spirit and comradeship of thousands of dojos of a hundred branches of Budo . . . the warrior skills. Bushido was not dead in Japan. It was perhaps now fulfilling its true purpose in a peace-loving nation.

~ chapter ten ~

Sasaki sempai had told me that a good way to strengthen the kicking muscles of legs and hips was to use the heavy iron clogs or "geta." They weigh seven pounds each, and are patterned after the traditional wooden footwear of Japan. The geta are held onto the feet by two straps that run along the sides of the feet and converge in a single strap that runs between the big toe and the second toe of each foot. When kicking with iron geta you must grip very hard with your toes to prevent the geta from flipping off. This strengthens the muscles of the feet far more than would the conventional iron boot of the Western body-builder. There was a martial arts shop a few hundred yards down from the Yotsuya subway station, where two army veterans made karategi, and sold various training devices for Karate. I bought a pair of iron geta, and began to use them at home.

At first I practiced slowly—front kicks, side snapping kicks, side thrust kicks, back kicks, roundhouse kicks, and I found that it was the muscles of my hips, and not the muscles of my legs, that became tired first.

"Ah, yes," said Sasaki, "your legs are strong, for you run quite well and fast, but they are long, and when there is a weight at the furthest extreme—the foot—great strain is placed on the point of insertion which is your hip. How many times have you been corrected for standing with your hips too high? You must practice with your hips low, and thus build strength in them. The teachers always tell us that we must have strength in the hips. You see how true it is. Keep practicing with the iron geta, but try to perform full and perfect movements, and after you have used them you must never omit to practice some fast kicks without them. This is very important, or you will develop strength, but no speed."

Within a month I could feel the increased power in my kicks. Also, I began to run with the iron geta lashed to my feet with strips cut from an old white belt, making tracks and crushing pebbles along the quiet lanes of Akitsu, past the fields bordered with tea hedges, past the roadside Buddhas, through the groves of chestnut trees.

Soon, I had passed the examination for the fifth kyu grade, and I wore the blue belt. From eating in a poor restaurant in Shibuya, I contracted dysentery and was hospitalized for three weeks. I lost a lot of weight. No longer was I a burly one hundred and ninety-five pounds. Already the hard training had stripped weight off me, but now I weighed only one hundred and seventy-five pounds. When I resumed training I was lighter and faster, but I had lost the kind of brute power that I had known before. Later, however, as I climbed the ranks, and the training became more concentrated, I would regain ten pounds. This weight, of one hundred and eighty-five pounds, would still remain constant ten years later, at the time of writing.

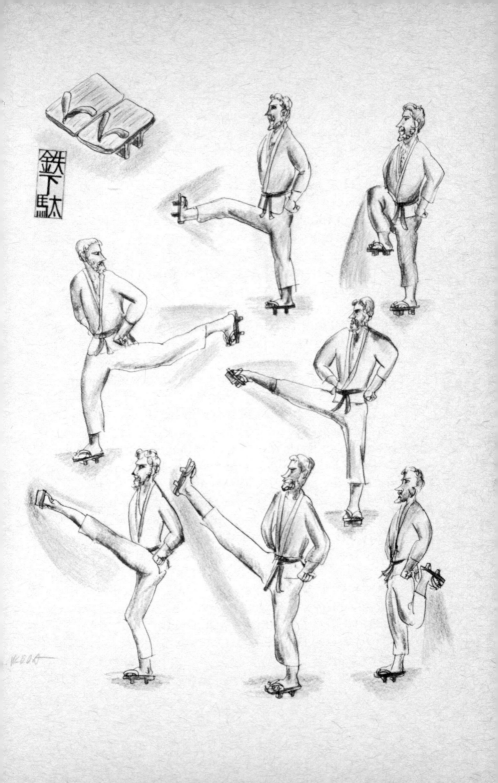

As a blue belt, I was still awkward and rather clumsy, still trying to get better stance. I was either too high in the hips, and thus wasting strength, or too low and stiff. Our grade was fair game for the rough fighting of the brown belts. They took it from their seniors, the first and second dan black belts, and in turn, they dished it out to us, with more than the required (in my opinion) ferocity. This was a period of much bruising of shins and forearms, a time of countless defeats and few victories, but it was also a time for steeling the determination.

I trained hard and passed the fourth kyu test. I still wore the purple belt, for both fourth and fifth kyu grades wore it, but I had taken examinations in all five of the Heian kata. From these kata we learned all the major defensive techniques. Now I had to learn the powerful kata of Tekki, the forms of armor-clad warriors, deep and strong in the "horse" or "straddle-stance." This kata developed strength in the inner thighs, legs and abdomen, and great speed in hand techniques.

On reaching fourth kyu, I knew that the brown belt, rank of third kyu, was within reach. I trained hard to fight, challenged my seniors repeatedly, forgot all fear of being defeated. It had taken me longer than usual to climb the first three grades, for I had concentrated on developing a strong punch and kick, and had neglected the practice of kata. But no longer did I neglect them. To run with sincerity through the five Heian kata was exhausting and exhilarating, but only a warm-up to diligent practice of Tekki. Sasaki, Okuda and Seto, my three friends and sempai, were leaning hard on me. Seto especially, who was rather small even for a Japanese, delighted in free fighting with me, again and again making me look like an overgrown child, punishing me without mercy with his lightning-fast kicks and savage in-fighting. They would destroy me, and then coach me to regain my confidence and fighting spirit. How fine it would be, I thought, to be able to fight like them! I especially admired Sasaki's style. He was long and lithe, and not much shorter than I. He kicked with grace and speed, and with his second dan grade he made short work of even the toughest first dan black belts.

True to his promise, Mr. Kanazawa was now giving me personal instruction. I went to the dojo an hour earlier than usual, three days a week, and during this hour he would coach me, alone, and for this he refused any kind of remuneration. Knowing that one of the best teachers in Japan was doing this for me made me work harder, sometimes coming almost to the point of tears when my body could not perform as he had instructed and shown me.

One morning, I went to the dojo early, but found it locked. This was odd, because Kanazawa sensei had told me to come, and from inside I could hear the sound of training. I looked through the glass panes in the rickety door, and could see that the office was functioning. I waited ten minutes, and Kanazawa sensei came to the door and let me in. He was in uniform, and sweating. He told me to be very quiet, to go into the waiting room and sit there, not to move or do anything. This was one of the training sessions for teachers and apprentice instructors, and students were locked out.

From the unlighted, gloomy changing room I could look out onto the dojo, where a few instructors were practicing kata. The main session was over, but Mr. Yaguchi, a very stern and tough teacher, was sparring with my friend Sasaki. Sasaki was receiving special training to bring him up to third dan rank and to prepare him for the role of teacher. He was going to go to the Philippines to teach Karate there.

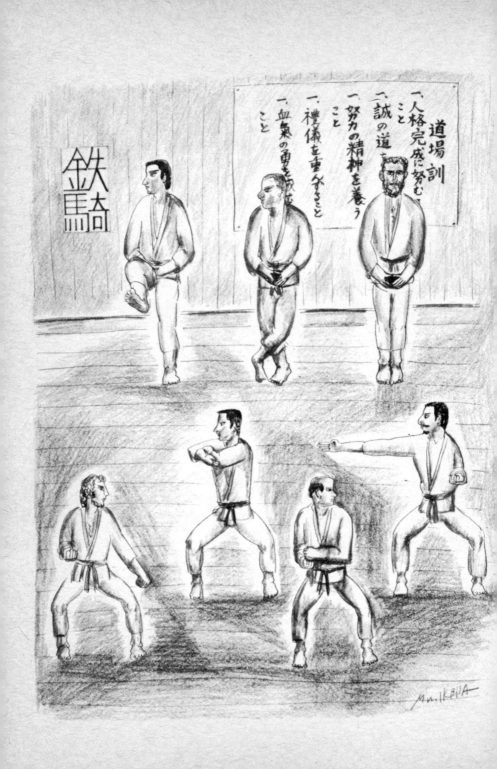

Now, the usually lithe and vigorous Sasaki, who could defeat first dan and most of the second dan black belts with ease, was staggering like a drunkard on the dojo floor. His techniques were slow and weak. He would try to kick, but lose his balance. Unthinkable! Yaguchi sensei was berating him, attacking him at the same time with seemingly casual techniques that smacked against his body, focused shallow enough not to damage, but stinging, and leaving red marks on the skin.

"Sasaki! What is this? What kind of technique is that? Fight! Find your spirit!"

Bang! He foot-swept my senior to the floor and thrust a kick at his chest.

"Get up, Sasaki! Come on!"

Sasaki got up, but was immediately swept to the ground again. He staggered back to his feet, and seemed to find the energy to attack the teacher with a round-house kick, ridge-hand attack combination, followed by a flurry of punches. With nonchalance, his attacks were parried and deflected. Bang! Down he went again.

"Sasaki! Your balance! It's horrible! Get up!"

Sasaki once more staggered to his feet, barely having enough strength to keep his hands higher than his waist. Yaguchi sensei gave a curt bow and walked away from him, and another teacher, Mr. Yajima, took over.

"Come on, Sasaki! A little longer."

From one end of the dojo, Mr. Nakayama watched, his face without expression. Despite himself, tears were coursing down my senior's cheeks, tears of exhaustion and frustration. His spirit rallied again and he lunged forward in a kicking and thrusting attack, only to be blocked again and again. I knew that it was not right that I should see my senior thus defeated. Although he could not discern me in the gloom of the changing room,

I bowed toward him and went out into the office. Ya-guchi sensei came out and looked sharply at me, as if to ask why the hell I was in the dojo now. Mr. Kanazawa interceded, then addressed me.

"We are breaking him down so that we can help him build his spirit. He has fought hard, with no rest, for more than one hour. Quite a time ago he thought that it was impossible for him to continue, but still he continues, and he will continue for another ten minutes. In a few days he will feel great pride in himself, and know that it is his spirit, and not his body, that makes the rules. He has fought very well." The teacher stressed this, and in his eyes he showed that he wanted me to understand that I must have respect for my sempai. I did. At the end of the session he would have fought a succession of skilled fighters for twice as long as any professional world boxing champion in a title match—and this without any rest at all.

Later, after a cold shower, Sasaki was dragging on his clothes. One of the young teachers brought him tea and put it before him.

"Ah, Nic-san, so ashamed am I that you should see me thus, helpless as a baby."

I replied that I felt nothing but admiration for him. He nodded tiredly, and Kanazawa sensei ordered me out onto the dojo floor. We had only thirty minutes before the main lesson, but he seemed to cram two hours of training into that short time.

The Japanese have a saying: "When a nail sticks up, knock it down!" When a student is good, becoming bet-ter than his fellows, his pride must be destroyed, he must be driven without mercy so that his spirit and skill will not suffer from conceit. The Karateka must con-stantly stretch himself to the utmost, so that once again, and again and again, he feels the helplessness of a baby.

Humility is an essential characteristic of the true warrior. Without it he has no place in society. He is a dangerous, ugly brute without humility. In defeat, he learns that still he can continue, and this teaches him spirit, and respect for others.

But in Karate, nobody is as arrogant and full of self-pride as the brown belt. It seems that the art pushes him up a hill of arrogance and conceit in his strength, just so that he might be toppled, far, far down. I was going to find out all about that.

Within two months of Mr. Kanazawa's coaching, I had learned the movements of the Tekki kata quite well. Mr. Kanazawa, being a tall, long-limbed man, taught full, graceful and powerful forms, and I had begun to gain great pleasure from practicing them.

One day, while practicing the Tekki kata, I became aware of Takagi sensei watching me. When I finished, he called me over.

"Nicol, you are improving, but the end of your kata is not good. When the movements of a kata are finished, you must have 'zanshin.' Do you know what that is?"

"I think so, sensei—it means 'perfect finish.' "

"Yes, it does, but what exactly is a perfect finish? Zanshin is comprised of two characters. The first one, 'zan,' means to remain, to continue. The second one, 'shin,' means heart or mind. When the movements of a kata are finished, do not think that the kata is finished, do not relax your attention and spirit. You must come to the closing position, keep your eyes ahead, your body and spirit ready for anything. You must be aware of all that is around you. Kata is not just a practice of movements, and neither is it a way of retreating into your own self. When you practice kata you must be acutely aware. You must have a mind like still water, reflecting all things. Finish your kata with zanshin, otherwise, no matter how brilliantly you perform it, it will be considered a failure."

From then on, I watched the teachers and high ranking black belts much more closely when they finished their kata. Their performance of kata flowed, and the flow of the kata did not end with the cessation of body movement. How difficult to catch this feeling, to explain it!

In perfect stillness, they exuded strength. I saw it, and I thought of herons, poised above a pool, ready to spear a fish; of high-soaring falcons ready to stoop; of a cat, sitting patiently by a mouse hole; or indeed, of an Eskimo hunter I'd known named Akeeago, poised, ready, yet totally relaxed, waiting for a seal to come up a breathing hole in the ice. And yet, even as these images came to my mind, I became confused. Zanshin was not these, for although they too were images of strength in stillness, these were all of the "before." What my teachers demonstrated at the end of a kata was strength in stillness, yet more, more. I try to pin it down with words and it eludes me. "Perfect finish" . . . "remaining spirit" . . . they will have to do.

With lower-ranking belts, even with most brown belts, the flow was cut off when the kata movements were completed, like a clockwork doll that had suddenly been switched off. Without good "kamae" or readiness at the beginning of the kata, and without zanshin at the end, the kata was only a physical exercise, and not a moving practice of Zen.

Once aware of the existence of this feeling, this continuation of spirit, I began to see it in other Japanese arts and customs; in the tea ceremony and in flower arranging, in classical Noh dancing, or in that exquisite moment of silence after the last notes of a fine piece of music had faded into nothingness.

At first, I found it impossible to achieve this "continuing spirit" or "perfect finish," and I resorted to mental tricks. With the movements of the kata finished, I would stand in the final position, eyes ahead, body motionless—then I would run through the kata again in my mind. When the mental rerun had finished, I would relax and bow out. From an onlooker's point of view it seemed effective enough, although I knew that it was not the real thing. But it would do for the moment.

Months passed. I became stronger, practices harder. On Sundays I practiced sword and discussed philosophy with my new friend Ikeda, and a couple of times a week I began to go to the Tomisaka police dojo to learn stick fighting with my wife, Sonako. It seemed no time at all before I was entitled to wear the brown belt.

I had been training almost two years now, and it was no longer easy for the younger and more inexperienced of the first dan black belts to beat me. Brown belts fought very hard and rough. We beat the lower ranks with an almost savage delight, and in our turn we were mercilessly beaten by our seniors, who now enjoyed contests with us, for we could give good account of ourselves, and force them into stronger defense and sharper attack. I had learned many techniques, and could execute them with a fair power, although how much power, I could not tell. We broke boards and tiles and took new delight in the calluses on our hands.

The days were long for me. I left early in the morning, traveling on the crowded trains to downtown Tokyo. After practice, I ate lunch with dojo friends.

In the afternoons I studied Japanese, or sometimes returned to the dojo, or sometimes went to learn stick fighting, or sometimes taught English conversation at a small school. I taught English in the evenings too. It was the most popular way for foreign, English-speaking students to earn enough money to live in Tokyo, which was, even in the early sixties, an expensive place to live. Rarely was it possible to get a seat on the train coming home, and I would hang from a strap with one hand, holding a paperback book in the other hand, bracing myself against the pressures of close-packed bodies all around me, lurching and swaying in the sardine-can carriages.

On one such journey, around nine at night, I was unfortunate enough to stand next to a very aggressive drunk. He was a laborer, muscular and brown, a small towel twisted and looped around his head, hair crewcut, small stubbly beard. He was about forty years old, sober enough to stand, but too drunk to keep his dislike of foreigners to himself. As the crowded carriage swayed and lurched, he kept up a continual muttering, loud enough for me, and for everybody else near us, to hear.

"In the war, we Japanese defeated them time and time again. They have no spirit. Only with atomic bombs could they defeat us. Trash! I am stronger than he is. Look at him! Why does he come to our country? Stupid fellow! Just his size is big, not his heart! And our girls like them! Huh! Trash! They're not Japanese girls, they are only whores!"

It was difficult, but I ignored him as did the other stony-faced Japanese in the carriage. They felt more embarrassed and uncomfortable than I did. At first I was not even angry, for by now I had become used to this kind of drunk. They were usually quite harmless.

But this one got bolder. The carriage lurched, and he took the opportunity to swing hard and jab his elbow upward at my ear. He was hanging onto the strap with both hands. After he hit me he glared malevolently.

"Cowards, all of them. See? I'm not afraid."

The carriage lurched again, and sure enough I got his right elbow in my left ear again. Very irritating. I put my book up on the luggage rack.

We had learned in the dojo that a blow under the armpit would cause great pain, and probably unconsciousness. A blow there from a master would cause death. In the Tekki kata we practiced close, hooking punches that started from the side of the body and passed in front of the striker's own chest. We practiced these powerful in-fighting blows with a partner, and learned how to deflect the opponent's arm upward, to expose the vulnerable underarm. In mounting anger, I now determined to test one of these techniques, just hard enough, or so I thought, to cause the bothersome drunk enough pain to make him drop his arm and quit jabbing me in the ear.

I waited for the next lurch, and as he began a jab at my ear I hooked a rising, close-bodied jab with my right fist, at the same time bracing my ankles, legs and abdomen, and deflecting his elbow upward with my left hand. The punch went deep into his armpit, and to my great surprise he dropped, falling in a heap on the lap of a gentleman who sat reading a newspaper directly in front of him. So crowded was the carriage that he could not fall and stretch out on the floor, but he was unconscious just the same. My fist had traveled less than eighteen inches. Minutes passed, and he lurched to his feet, grabbing at people standing there to help him up. I didn't know what to do, and said nothing, ready to hit him and anybody else if need be.

But he did nothing, and squeezed behind me and made his way to the exit, where he stood staring at the rubber-edged crack between the sliding pneumatic doors. At the next station he got off, and neither he, I, nor anybody else said a word.

On the station platform of Akitsu, I breathed a sigh of relief in the cool evening air. Hell, I didn't really think that the blow would knock him out! That rather unpleasant incident demonstrates why brown belts are more dangerous than dan ranks. I told myself I would not try out such a technique again unless my life depended on it. If Kanazawa sensei had heard about it, I would have been suspended from the dojo for at least six months.

◦ chapter eleven ◦

Before Kanazawa sensei came out onto the dojo floor, I was to perform the kata twenty times, "with spirit." He had chosen for me the long kata called "Kanku Dai," and this was to be performed for my black belt examination. It took about two minutes to complete it, for it is a long kata, with sixty-five movements, and so, to follow my teacher's instructions, I would have to perform forty minutes of kata before he came. This took at least an hour. Sometimes the dojo was locked when I arrived, and I did the kata outside, hampered by my tight Western clothes and by the narrowness of the alleyway.

It is a beautiful kata, begun by slowly raising the hands with forefingers and thumbs touching, and gazing at the emptiness of the sky through the small triangular "window" thus formed. The movements of the kata are deep, long and expressive, and it ends with a spectacular double flying kick. By repeating the kata so many times, the sequence of the moves would become automatic, and my strength and stamina would be built up.

On his arrival, Kanazawa sensei would coach me first in the kata, never correcting more than two, and usually only one point at a time. He stressed fine form, correct breathing and proper application of power. At no time under his instruction did my head swim with things to remember, for he avoided flooding my mind with instructions. After the kata, we would practice basic movements, or kihon, and then combinations of techniques. Sometimes he would spar with me, dropping his speed so that I would not be overwhelmed and could thus practice blocking, parrying, moving, avoiding and attack. Once in a while he would unleash his truly incredible speed and agility. With apparent ease, he could leap over my head from the front, kick at the back of my neck, strike at my spine, and move out of range before I could turn around. From a front stance, he could lunge fifteen feet across the dojo, reaching my face with his fist before I could even react to his movement and attempt to block it. He was infinitely faster and more skilled than I, yet he was always gentle and respectful of my feelings and my person. With fine techniques, including throws sometimes, he would defeat me, but even in defeat, he always allowed me my dignity, never did he throw in that extra technique, the obvious one, that demonstrated mastery. No movement was showy or wasted. Rarely had I felt such respect, not out of physical fear, or even out of gratitude or admiration. I respected Kanazawa sensei for his gentleness. This is what I had come to seek.

Takagi sensei had been watching, and while we finished the private lesson one morning, he smiled at me. It was a month before the black belt examination.

"You have come to like and to understand kata. That is good. You are at the doorway now. Practice diligently and enter deeply."

He turned to my mentor. "What do you think? Can he succeed?"

"Yes, he can. There are still weak points which require much polishing, but his progress is steady and earnest."

"You have greatly aided him. His spirit is ready for the first step."

"Yes indeed."

I overheard this and felt tremendous joy, and determined to train harder, harder, so that I would not disappoint my teachers.

Many things were becoming clearer in my mind. Among these was the business of "kiai." At first, I had learned to give a shout at certain points during the kata, usually at two points. This shout, I had surmised, was similar to the grunt a man gave when he lifted a heavy object or swung an axe into a tough log. I was right, but not completely. I then learned strange things about this yell. It was written that superb swordsmen, especially those who meditated alone in the mountain, could give vent to a yell that would bring flying birds out of the sky, or immobilize a foe. Truly, while sparring with Mr. Kanazawa, I had been stopped dead in my tracks when the yell was given. I had seen other teachers do it to other students. I had seen it in the Kendo dojo, and in the dojo of the women who practiced with the "naginata"—the mowing halberd. I thought then that the purpose of kiai was to strike fear into an opponent. But this was a wrong assumption. The study of Japanese characters gave me some clue to the meaning of kiai. The first character, 気 , "ki," is the symbol for spirit, mind, energy, force. The second character, 合, "ai," is the symbol for meeting, or coming together. "The coming together of mind"—what could this mean?

Kiai is applied at focal points of the kata or of the combat sequence. It occurs as great power is put into a movement, and when it does so, the muscles of the body, especially those of the diaphragm, contract very strongly. Air is forced out of the lungs by this contraction, and a loud shout is made. But the shout is not of itself the object of the exercise. Many Western Karateka misunderstand this. The bang of a gun is a result of the explosion, and the explosion is a means of transforming energy from one form to another. We do not fire a gun to make a bang, and neither do we "kiai" to make a shout. The shout is the product of the kiai, and this is a central truth. The kiai then, is a moment of great focus of body and mind. "Kiai" is applied in all of the Japanese martial arts, and especially in sword ways, where a split instant, much too fast for the normal span of time required for sight to nerve-impulse to understanding to brain-command to nerve impulse to reaction, could mean infinity.

If "kamae" is "readiness," when the mind is like the moon, shining calmly on all—then "kiai" is a convergent laser of awareness and action.

In studies of sword and stick, later confirmed by my Karate teachers, I learned that there were right and wrong sounds associated with kiai. The three most usual, and correct sounds, are Ei! Ya! and Oh! The correct application of a given sound is a very difficult and technical subject, but in general, what mattered was the manner by which air was allowed to pass out of the body. Long, drawn out, shrieking, animalistic screams, so popular in the mass of fiction about martial arts, are not "true kiai." They are only shouts.

Therefore, the kata begins when the mind is opened, with "kamae" or readiness. It is calmness and latent energy. Then the kata flows, and the body is

moved as a log is carried in a river. The kata is punctuated by "kiai" when body, mind and energy meet at a focal point. It is finished with zanshin, when the body has ceased to move, but energy still flows. Kata is stillness and movement, form that fills emptiness, piercing sound and silence, strength and gentleness. Kata is moving Zen. No classical dance was ever more beautiful than perfect kata.

Of course, I still used the "hard" training methods. My hands and feet were so strong now that I could strike the unpadded makiwara with all my force and feel no pain. No Japanese, glancing at my hands, would miss the fact that I was a Karateka. I used the makiwara, the iron geta, barbells, the heavy wooden practice sword, but I also had learned new methods.

A lighted candle was set up, and with focus, you struck at it, stopping the blow just short of the flame. If the focus had been good, the air displaced by the fist would puff out the flame. It sounds easy, but it is quite hard to do it consistently. The fist must not pass by the flame, or pass through it. Only when the fist filled space suddenly would the air puff out the flame. This method greatly helped focus. A similar thing could be done with hanging sheets of paper, trying to tear the paper by snapping back the fist, sucking air so that the paper got torn.

Especially in the blue and early brown belt ranks, I had tried my strength by breaking boards and tiles. This spectacular, crowd-pleasing series of tricks, so often mistaken as the major part of Karate, is actually very little stressed in most of the good schools. Most of us do it, to see if we can, and I was no exception. But the real test of breaking power was to break a single board (teachers can break two or three together this way) that is hanging free. A blow of massive power will not necessarily break the board, and neither will a blow that has only speed. The blow must have speed and focus, correct application of power, for the free-hanging board to break. I tried many times and failed, but at long last, I began to succeed.

Karate training had also helped me to bear pain. Perhaps "bear" is not the right word. "Bearing" implies a stoical endurance, a gritting of the teeth, a special courage. No. I had begun to learn to "see" pain, to recognize it, to know it, to realize its value as a warning signal, and then to override it if I so wished. A shin is bruised badly, but the match is not finished. The mind sees the injury and appreciates it for what it truly is—a signal from one part of the body, not a total destruction of psyche. My teacher, Kanazawa, had won the All Japan Karate championships with a broken arm. However, total disassociation from pain would be very dangerous, and the Karateka does not do this. Karate training had begun—only just begun, mind you—to teach me calmness.

The same ability to "see" and appreciate would help with exhaustion, hunger, heat, cold. All these things I could take better now, and this was not only the result of my improved strength, stamina and energy. I believe that it was the first glimmerings of "ki" or spirit. The martial artist must regard his body as a splendid tool for the spirit to use. The body should not be allowed to dominate the spirit.

Most importantly for me, Karate had begun to teach me to control my very violent emotions. Before I had practiced Karate I had been physically strong, but emotionally weak. With rudiments of Judo and Jujitsu, and with a year of professonal wrestling, I had been a street fighter. In one year I had eleven serious street fights. In those days I would feel anger rising, anger mixed with terror. I would try to suppress it, like stoppering a water-filled bottle on a fire. It always ended in an explosion. But with Karate training I had learned to recognize the stirring of rage in my bowels, and had been taught how to quell it with gentle breathing and tension of the abdomen, and then to relax body and mind and allow rage to dissolve into nothingness. An angry Karateka is easily defeated. We all knew that. Rage, hate, passionate love, these are all created within ourselves, and we are truly weak if we cannot control them.

Please do not think that I claim that Karate made me a spiritual master, a yogi, a saint. Certainly not. Weakness of spirit would torment me all my life, but Karate had given me the means to control, understand, and contain it. It was very rare now for me to "lose" my temper.

As a white belt, temper had gone from me, and I had fought with rage. Through the ranks of the colored belts I had learned to subdue temper. As I approached black belt, I had just begun to recognize temper and let it dissolve.

When anger knots the guts, a good and simple way to get rid of it is to transfer this nervous energy and frustration to the makiwara or punching bag. However, practice of kata is a much better and surer way. Mental tricks helped too; if I was hurt by an insult, or by the ignorance or thoughtlessness of others, I could act out a fantasy in my mind. In this fantasy I could strike, kick, throw, twist, kill or maim the person responsible. But by no means did I let the fantasy end there. I would imagine him lying injured, and imagine the nature of the injury that could be inflicted by this or that technique. I would see the logical follow-through of all this —shocked bystanders, blood, police, ambulance. I would see myself being arrested and charged, facing the victim again in court, or facing his relatives and loved ones. I would see myself being deported from Japan, expelled from the dojo, my wife's disgust and my teachers' disappointment. I would see grief, hate, pain, shame, all caused by my attack. No! No!

I had to overcome my schoolboy notions of honor and courage. I had to learn to know when a situation was developing, to seek to avoid it, or to turn it from its course. Finally, I had begun to learn, especially from Kanazawa sensei, that if it became essential to fight and overcome an attacker, then it was permissible to defeat, but evil to humiliate.

"Hitotsu! Kekki no yu o imashimuru koto!"

The fifth tenet of the dojo oath—"One! To guard against impetuous courage!"

The "kara" or emptiness of Karate also implied an ability to receive the feelings and state of mind of others, to reflect others. I knew now that our training was ultimately aimed at this.

I was fighting Seto, my sempai. It was after class, and we were relaxed. He is small, but very fast, and he teased me for my size and relative slowness. I charged, and grabbed hold of him, meaning to lift him off the ground in a wrestling throw. From between my arms, his leg shot out in a side thrust kick that caught me under the heart and hurled my body, much heavier than his, against the wall. Gasping, trying hard to breathe, I felt panic, and feared slipping into unconsciousness. My chest muscles refused to work.

"Nic-san. Relax. Breathe with your abdomen, push it down, find strength in your abdomen."

I remembered, and breathed again, and the cramp-

ing passed with the panic. Hours later, I did not even have bruised ribs. Seto admonished me.

"Ah! No good! You forget! Focus your body when the blow comes, and meet it with your spirit if you are unable to block. You see? You were holding me, and your hands were fixed like that. It was easy to kick you. But you should have focused your spirit against the attack you must have known would come!"

"Sempai, I forgot."

"Forgot! That is no good! Come on, again!"

We bowed to each other and he immediately kicked me in the same spot, focusing very shallow, so that no damage should be done to my body if it was unprepared. But this time I remembered, and the blow only left a red mark on my chest that soon faded.

Very often, a victim of a blow is not actually injured seriously by the force of the blow alone; he can harm himself greatly by panic and by violent contractions. He can even kill himself this way, and every Karate instructor should be prepared to deal with this sort of thing. (Sadly, outside of Japan, most instructors do not have the least idea of how to deal with it.)

With good muscle tone, good stance, proper breathing, awareness and focus, a Karateka can withstand body blows that would cripple another, untrained man.

The Tekki kata are excellent as an early training method to develop this. These kata are of the hard, powerful, "Shorei" school, and they develop great strength in abdomen and chest. Internal strength is especially developed.

Within a month of the black belt examinations, Kanazawa sensei taught me another very dynamic kata of the Shorei school. This one, called "Hangetsu" or "half moon," because of the peculiar stepping motions, had very slow, very strong, "dynamic tension" type of movements, punctuated by extremely fast and powerfully focused hand techniques. This kata taught the practitioner to be able to exert great force, to harden his body, to move slowly, and then, in an instant, to relax, move like a striking snake, then become hard again. It was a "hard-soft-hard" kata, very difficult for me. It taught two new stances that required especial strength in hips and inner thighs.

Mr. Kanazawa also taught me a kata called "Bassai Dai" or "to penetrate a fortress." This one, like the long kata of "Kanku Dai," was of the Shorin school, and had large, fluid movements. It was probably the most popular kata for aspiring brown belts, and it emphasized a continual shifting to advantageous position to block an opponent's powerful attacks.

I believe that Kanazawa sensei wanted my training to be balanced between these two major schools, which had been blended by the old Okinawan masters to become our present style.

Now, after two years of training, it no longer seemed incongruous that such a deadly art should have largely sprung from ancient temples, mostly Chinese, thence to be modified by men who were among the finest philosophers of their time.

When I came to Japan I had been very heavily muscled, and had thought then that this strength of muscle and sinew would enable me to withstand almost anyone who wanted to punch me in the stomach. For ordinary men, it was a fair assumption. But in the Karate dojo I soon learned that a small, light man like my friend Seto could cripple me with a Karate punch, whose power would explode inside my body if my spirit were not prepared. Thick, hard, tensed muscle was not adequate protection.

When a blow comes, and you tense your body,

thinking that the body is so hard that it cannot be harmed, then like as not, the shock will travel through the tensed muscles and harm internal organs or cause massive bruising within the muscle itself. In the legends of Karate there are many stories of "delayed death blows." Personally, I came to believe that what I have described above was what happened in many of the cases of a "delayed death blow." The blow might have little visible effect at the time of delivery, but it caused death at a later date. The person who hardens his body, believing that physical strength will protect him, has fear within him. He has made presumptions. Moreover, that very rigidity of muscle, bone and sinew in his body can cause it to transmit the shock waves of a fast, focused blow. This is not the course an advanced Karateka takes. He learns to be hard, and then soft. He must have dual nature of steel and water.

Naturally, the best defense against a blow is to avoid it, parry it, or block it. Yet sometimes a blow is inevitable, and although we see it, we cannot move to stop it. In this case, the Karateka should not merely tense up. He should "meet" the blow with his "ki" or spirit. Physically speaking, it seems that just as the blow reaches the surface of the body and begins to unleash its power, the body is not hard, but relaxed. Thus the initial part of the blow is absorbed by relaxed tissues, by softness. Then, as the blow continues to penetrate, the body becomes iron-hard, and the blow, already half-spent, is repulsed. Strong men have been injured, in wrist and elbow, while attempting to strike a person who is able to do this.

However, to do this well requires many years of practice, and no novice should experiment! It requires a strong, finely-controlled body, great calmness and confidence and superb timing. Unfortunately, it seems nearly impossible to focus one's testicles against attack! There, as for head, spine and a few vital points, you *must* avoid or block!

From the ranks of white belt to brown, my body had been trained to harden and relax in very short periods of time. At brown belt level, I was ready to begin to focus my body against a blow and meet an attack with my spirit. It had taken two years of hard training. And yet still I often forgot to do this, and got badly winded by the savage attacks of my seniors.

After training, the long Tokyo day, and crowded trains, it was sheer bliss to get home and take a Japanese bath. Like all Japanese men, I had come to think of the bath as an essential part of my daily routine. To wash off, and then sit in hot, clean water up to my chin was heaven. I came out clean, relaxed and warmed through to the bones. And after that, an earthenware bottle of warmed sake to please the palate and titillate the senses.

Does it need to be said that the Karateka is not considered a true warrior and a gentleman unless he keeps his body clean?

∽ chapter twelve ∽

It was November, and in the cold of the morning we began our waiting, crowded so close to each other that we touched, knee to knee, feeling discomfort change to pain, pain to numbness as we knelt in straight and silent lines on the wooden floor of the dojo. At first, the cold penetrated the thin cotton uniforms, but then, even of that, we became unaware.

Three tables were set out on the dojo floor, and at each table sat three teachers, solemn, stern, noticing the least fidget in the lines of waiting students. Two hundred students were to take the test that day, and I was the only Caucasian. And yet never had I felt so Japanese, so much a part of it all, sharing the fears, apprehensions, hopes and discomforts of my comrades. As each name was called out, I felt a jolt in my stomach.

Kihon. Basic moves. In pairs, the students were called, and they rose from their kneeling position, stepped forward, bowed to the flag and to the picture of Gichin Funakoshi, bowed to the teachers, and stood in the position of readiness.

"Gedan barai!" Downblock, stepping to the forward stance. Knees stiff from the long kneeling. As a teacher ordered them, the students performed all of the basic blocks. Downblock, rising block, inner block, outer block, knife-hand block, cross blocks, augmented blocks. Then they were ordered to perform the basic punching and striking techniques—reverse punch, forward lunging punch, hammer fist, back fist, knife hand, ridge hand, elbow strikes. Following that came the kicks— front snap kick, front thrust kick, side snap kick, side thrust kick, back kick, roundhouse kick. Each individual move had to be precisely and clearly performed, with no jerkiness or loss of balance.

"Yes, return to your place and wait."

Again, the pair of students bowed to the teachers, the front, and returned to their waiting, kneeling position. No student was allowed to speak. Teachers gave no sign of either approval or disapproval. We waited.

"Student Nicol!"

I stepped up, bowed, stood ready. There was no sensation in my legs, knees or ankles. My body seemed to end at the hips, and only determination kept me from falling down. All apprehension was gone. Between the beginning and the end of the movements, no time passed. As ordered, I bowed, returned to my position and waited.

The polished wooden floor was hard and unyielding, but it imparted a stream of memories. In order to overcome the numbness of waiting and kneeling, I had begun to breathe in tune to my heart beat, inhaling and exhaling to the count of fifteen heart beats. It became a song within me, an internal solo that moved my consciousness on a gentle returning wave. Images, sounds and feelings moved in those waves, spanning over two years in this small, poorly-lit place. Sometimes my mind sought to escape from the Now of the dojo and of waiting, but gently, firmly, I guided it back, soundlessly repeating the dojo oath in my head, finding that the unspoken words of Japanese became part of the soft intake and outpush of breath and the steady beat of my heart.

. . . My friends, the American called Gary Frederick and the young teacher, Anki Takahashi. They moved across this floor, practicing a powerful pushing block that stopped a punch as it began to move from the opponent's shoulder . . . sudden realization, unconnected to the mind image of memory, of how much Takahashi had done to nurture my curiosity. He was a Buddhist scholar. Yes, I remembered how we had discussed the book *The Little Prince* which I had lent to him, knowing he would like it. The flower. The fox. Talks about Japanese poetry. Image of the god Komokuten. Flashes of memory of Nakayama sensei as he parried the club I swung at his head. Takahashi could fight like a demon-god, yet never did I see an expression of violence on his face. Bullet Head. Was it in this dojo that I flew into a rage? Unthinkable. Personalities passed before my mind, a stream of them. The one-armed man who pinned his empty sleeve to his chest. The sixty-year-old business man who trained so hard. The man who limped, yet who chose the most difficult kata for footwork. The German who tried to throw Okuda and was thrown in turn. So many students, so many struggles. In the present, the kiai of the performing students rang sharp and clear. I gazed straight ahead, but through my peripheral vision I could see a couple of lines of the dojo oath. Behind me, hundreds of little wooden name plates, all of students who had knelt here, like us, and who passed their test.

. . . Last year, at New Year, and at early training,

they made a shrine, decorated with hard, white, round rice cakes, with boughs of pine, of plum and of bamboo. Seto broke the cakes with a punch, and we had them toasted over charcoal, or softened in sweet soup. We had various kinds of pickles and small fish, rice cooked with red beans, sake, and good wishes for the New Year . . . Sounds of training at the makiwara, students counting the punches, steady as heart beats. Steam from the kettle that made tea for the teachers. Smells of sweat and old wood. Now I remembered it! On first being in the dojo I had felt a strange uneasiness, despite the friendliness of the people there. It faded soon enough, and I had thought that I had been a little uncomfortable because I was foreign, and spoke no Japanese. Now I realized that it had been caused by the steady, unwavering gaze of the Karateka. They looked straight into a newcomer's eyes, without hostility or curiosity. That was unnerving, but soon I had become trained to do it. It was a habit that became reinforced by others who shared it. In the dojo we shared a life and death ritual, one that required the utmost trust and control. The eyes mirrored any instability, they telegraphed vicious or fearful intentions. Still gazing straight ahead, I observed how the teachers looked steadily at the performing students, their glances falling away only to write notes on the sheets of paper before them.

We were aware of the seriousness of our testing. It was of the utmost importance that each student performed his best, showed with honesty what he knew. If we failed, it would mean that we needed further training before attaining the first dan rank. We all sought to know. We waited. Hours passed.

Once again my name was called. I rose, separating myself from the other-reality of numbed legs. This time it was the examination for kata. I bowed to the front, to the teachers, and took my place on the small white line which marked where the kata should begin, and where, after sixty-five steps, leaps, spins, stamps, lunges and kicks, where, exactly where, my feet should come to rest when the kata finished. Any ill-balanced steps at any point in the kata would betray me at the end. I spoke aloud the name of the kata I had chosen. Kamae. Consciously, I quietened my heart and breathing, opened my mind so the kata would take me when it chose to. Kata. My kiai knifing the quietness. Zanshin. As I surfaced again I was aware of all the small mistakes I had made, but I had returned to the little white line, and had performed to the best of my ability. I bowed, and returned to my place.

More waiting. Images continued to flow through my mind, myriads of them, blending yet not blurring into one long memory of the seconds, minutes, hours spent in this dojo. I was a part of the dojo. My personality permeated the walls and floor, mingled with the others. I was a valid, true, inseparable part of the stream of its being. I belonged here, along with all the others, and it no longer really mattered if I passed or failed the test this time.

"Student Nicol!"

I went up once more. The teachers called me to the center table. One of them held up a pencil. "Reverse punch at this pencil, at the tip, with power and focus. Punch each time the pencil stops."

He moved and stopped it quickly, six or seven times, and I followed with my punches. Sonako had washed my karategi, and it snapped against my arm, with a satisfactory crack.

"Back fist strike. Fast!"

He moved the pencil and I struck at it, watched

closely by the two teachers who flanked him, while the pencil-holding teacher watched my eyes. They repeated the test for the left side. If my control and timing had been bad I would have failed the entire examination, no matter how well I did in the other parts. Poor control could mean serious, perhaps fatal injury to one's partner.

"Good. Go over there."

I went over and stood beside another student. Together we bowed to the front and again to the teachers. At the command, we turned and bowed to each other. He was small, his head shaven close, his eyes glittering. We knew each other. He was one of the tougher brown belts from the Takushoku University club, the same group that had produced my old enemy Bullet Head. This guy was OK, if a bit wild. His hands were heavily callused, even on the palms, where calluses developed from very tight gripping of the fist. Had they put me against a Takushoku man for a reason? Images flashed through my mind—results of a hundred dojo fights, of many defeats and a few victories. Then, with crystal clarity, I remembered the warning which Seto and Okuda had given me before I came into the dojo this morning.

. . . "Nic-san. Do your best. Remember this, though. If you retreat one centimeter, just one little centimeter, we will be watching, we will see, and later we will beat you. You had better be more afraid of us than of your opponent. Don't forget that. It is no joke."

I remembered. I looked across at my opponent and saw that he was excited. Suddenly, the command! He rushed forward at me, giving vent to a yell, kicking and punching. In one deep, long movement I executed a thrusting punch to the jaw, and as my arms were longer than his, it served to stop his attack. Point! It was a clean technique, and I had not retreated. I do not remember the other attacks too well, except that one of them I countered with a sharp, snapping knife hand to my opponent's neck, and two teachers argued briefly about it, one saying it would not have been effective, and the other two saying it would. I said nothing, of course, but I knew that the technique was effective enough, even if my delivery was not perfect. They counted it. Soon, it was finished and we were in our places in the crowded, kneeling lines again.

On that day, two hundred students were examined for their first dan rank. Eighty of them passed. The long, long waiting of that day seemed to span only a few minutes, a quick flash of impressions. The day was over. We were able to bow out of the dojo, to change into warm clothes, to go to the toilet, to drink water, to go eat and drink with our friends.

"Nic-san, you did well, good, good!" Seto slapped me on the back. My fighting partner rushed up. "It was good, don't worry!" He was grinning, shaking my hand. I knew he had passed. I had seen his examinations for basics and kata, and he performed them very well. The teachers would have given him good marks too for his fighting spirit and sharp, hard techniques. We grinned at each other, promised to drink sake with each other sometime soon. He was called away by his senior students, and he bowed and left me. I saw that Bullet Head was there, he looked over at me, into my eyes and smiled, a good, friendly smile, then he nodded, as if to say that everything was fine. Had I passed? Could I dare to hope? I pushed the question out of my mind.

The next day the dojo was occupied with tests for higher ranks. At home Sonako and I said very little about the examination. The more I thought about it, the more my various weaknesses came back to me, and I began to prepare myself for word that I had failed.

As usual, I arrived for training early. Kanazawa sensei was discussing something with Takagi sensei when I stepped up onto the wooden floor, put my shoes into the box, and bowed.

"Ah, student Nicol! How are you today? Are you well?"

"Thank you sensei. I am well."

Takagi sensei stood up and squeezed out from behind the desk, his hand outstretched. Kanazawa sensei. was grinning like a Cheshire cat.

"Well done! Congratulations!"

He shook my hand. A great surge of joy came to my heart, and I mumbled thanks to both of them.

"Your certificate will be presented to you when we move to the new dojo. Go and train now. Now the real training begins. This is the last time you will be wearing a brown belt. Go now, hurry, train hard!"

For the last time, I bowed into the dojo as a brown belt, a kyu rank. I had passed! Banzai!

~ chapter thirteen ~

The headquarters of the Japan Karate Association moved to Suidobashi, a couple of stations down the Chuo line, past Ichigaya with its fish ponds, and past the old house on the hill by the headquarters of the Self Defense Force, where I had lived with Donn Draeger, Bill Fuller and the others. The new dojo was upstairs in the former Kodokan building. It was much larger than the old one, and had better facilities. Why, it even had hot showers! There was a weight training club in the basement, where many of the Judo champions had trained. Yukio Mishima, the brilliant novelist and swordsman, used to train there, and in the future he was to win a first dan rank in Karate at our school before indelibly marking the pages of history with his abortive attempt at a coup d'etat and his death by ritual suicide and beheading.

The old Kodokan building is just a few yards from Suidobashi station, and the rumble of trains is constant. The air is not good there, and even in the space of two years and a few months, I had noticed the worsening of air pollution. The Korakuen amusement park was close by, and beyond that was the new Kodokan, where I had spent the first weeks of my stay in Japan.

That year, the year of the Tokyo Olympics, there was a movement to bring accord between the major schools of Karate. The JKA, Goju-ryu, Shito-ryu and Wado-ryu were having many meetings. Inspired by the Olympics, and by the very successful introduction of Judo as an Olympic event, they had an eye to the possibility of future Karate competitions on a world level. This was excellent. It came to mean that the major schools would recognize and honor each other's ranks and would pave the way for future accord on a hundred different points. Although the competition and squabbling were to go on for at least another decade, it was now possible to exchange ideas as well as challenges and insults. Until this time, the ranks of all our teachers had been kept low, never going higher than fifth dan. Funakoshi sensei had been fifth dan, and nobody wanted to be ranked higher. However, after these meetings, ranks were raised to a higher and more realistic level in order to correspond to their fellows in other major schools.

Kyokushinkai, Mas Oyama's school, which is also very big in Japan, did not take part in this amalgamation into a national Karate body. Not being aware of the ramifications of interschool politics, I could only presume that this was due to his own fierce individualism.

By this time, by the time of the move, I did not possess one black belt, but three, all representing the same dan rank. Anki Takahashi had given me one with my name embroidered in red on one side, and his name on the other. Seto had given me one with my nickname ("Nic") embroidered in orange on one side and his name on the other. Sasaki had also given me one, embroidered with white, with my name transcribed into the Japanese characters for "Nikko," which means "sunshine," because, he said, that I smiled a lot, like a child. Having been given three belts presented me with an awful problem. I could not wear all three at once, yet I wanted to show my appreciation. However, it seemed to me that it was a cycle of fate that I had come from the Arctic to Japan, and that the Eskimo people I had known on my first two expeditions to the Arctic had given me a name which means "little boy who smiles." Therefore I decided to wear Sasaki's belt at first, while in Japan. Later, I would rotate the belts. It seems a silly problem, but really, it was quite serious!

No matter which of the three new black belts I chose to wear, the results of stepping onto the dojo floor as a new dan rank would have been the same. A dozen of my seniors were there, including Sasaki and the powerful German black belt, Herman Kauz. Sasaki was first, with a smile, with congratulations, and with a request, very polite, to spar. After hitting the floor for the twentieth time, the hurt didn't seem to matter very much. Only the awful fatigue, the painful heaving of my lungs, the sweat running down into my eyes and the absolute need to get up again and fight were the things that mattered. One after another the sempai fought me, defeating me repeatedly. The nail was being knocked down. My uniform became soaking wet, and dye from the new black belt stained it. I was profoundly grateful when the class was called to order.

I was prepared for this process of humiliation; otherwise it would have been unbearable. To watch senior students and teachers with new black belts you would think that they hated them. When we began to do Karate, then everything we did was wrong. With me it was hips, always hips—too high, or too low, or too something or other. When we were not actually practicing though, the senior students and teachers all congratulated and complimented us, even if the message, very clear, was that now we had to train in earnest.

"You have stepped into the door of the dojo now," said one teacher, berating me for having broken the position we had been holding for ten minutes, "and now, only just now, do we consider it worth our while to try to teach you. Therefore you will obey, show spirit, and work hard. What kind of a black belt has to worry about a little cramp?"

I did not try to say that I had been kicked in the back of the thigh before, and was beginning to get a charley horse.

Kase sensei gave us our first formal lesson, a special lesson in a series for new black belts. In his manner and speech he was always polite and kind, but in what he expected of us he was a tyrant. The first lesson? Heian shodan, the kata required for the eighth kyu grading, for white belt, the first kata we had ever learned. It was awful. Not one of us escaped being corrected on twenty-odd points. Again and again we repeated the kata. A few of us had omitted to practice the five Heian kata, so concerned were we with the kata of choice for the black belt examination. When we first began, some of us fumbled slightly even over the sequence of movements. Kase sensei broke the kata down, polished each little detail. It was very clear that we must keep on trying to perfect the basic kata. After one hour of this, Kase sensei told us to add front kicks to each change of stance, which meant an addition of twenty snapping kicks, all to head height, all delivered in the forty-five seconds that it took to complete the kata. How many times we did this I don't know, but I was sure that if he said "One more time!" just one more time, I was going to pass out. But nobody passed out. At the end of the lesson he lectured us on practicing basic kata, for in these was the integrity of our style preserved. He said that if we practiced for twenty years, we might be able to master about three of them. Between simple knowledge of a thing and mastery of that thing there is a wide gap.

A simple event was to take place to make me profoundly grateful to the imposition of such high standards. One morning, Nakayama sensei asked me to stay after classes and act as a sparring partner for a young man from the Philippines who had requested a special grading. He claimed that he had come to Japan especially to get his second dan rank, and could spend only a very short time in the country. A table was set up, and three senior teachers sat down at it. I was surprised to see the young man waiting on the dojo floor in his uniform, wearing a black belt. We had only just finished classes. Why did he not train with us, and get himself warmed up and ready for the test? I knelt off to one side, waiting for him to complete the first three parts of the examination. It was pathetic. He claimed to have been trained and graded in the Shotokan style, our style, in the Philippines, but nobody knew his teacher. When asked to do kata he didn't even know what we meant. With each kick he wobbled. His punches had no snap, no focus. He actually struck the pencil. I was called up to do the kumite part of the examination with him, and at my first attack he closed his eyes, as if afraid of what was coming.

"That is enough." Nakayama sensei acknowledged my bow and motioned me away. With patience, he got up and demonstrated just a few points, explaining to the would-be second dan that he was not really ready.

Second dan! He was not ready for green belt! He was very wise not to have practiced with us, because many of the young black belts would have wanted to spar with the stranger, and once finding him such a disgrace to his belt, they would have driven the lesson home very hard indeed.

I resolved that I would never seek a higher rank, or want a higher rank unless I was absolutely sure that I was worthy of it, and sure that I would be at least the equal of any other man in that rank, no matter what the style.

The stranger never returned, and was not charged for the examination. I couldn't help feeling contempt for him, but our chief instructor did not, he only shook his head. "Poor fellow," he said, with no trace of sarcasm, "he has not received adequate teaching."

By this time Sonako had also gained her first dan in Jojitsu. I wished we could spend another year in Japan, so that I could study at her dojo and learn more about this graceful art. Her teacher, Shimizu sensei, was now in his seventies, yet with a sweep of his white oak stick he could either knock the sword out of my hand, or spin my body off balance. What was the secret of these old men who were so vigorous and strong? Masters of the martial arts retained their vigor into their eighties and nineties, then, almost without exception, they died quietly and with dignity. Whatever it was, it was certainly more than mere physical exercise. They practiced "moving meditation." They could stop time, empty themselves of fears and stresses, become strong, become gentle.

The Year of the Dragon was drawing to an end. For me, it was the end of my second twelve-year cycle. Rat, ox, tiger, dragon, snake, horse, sheep, monkey, rooster, dog, boar. Twenty-four years before I had been born in Wales, whose national flag bore the emblem of the red dragon. It seemed to me that I had been born and reborn under the dragon. This year, 1964, had been an auspicious year for me, a year in which I had achieved one of my greatest ambitions; achieved it, and then found it to be only a beginning, so that in the achieving of it there lay no anticlimax, only a step into newness. Two twelve-year cycles of my life had been completed, and from our neighbor, the fletcher, I received a symbolic gift of a fine war arrow inscribed with the dragon character, and with the shaft and flights newly made, but the head of the arrow the work of a steel master, a sword maker, a valuable point that was centuries old.

Soon we would pass into the Year of the Snake, and Sonako and I would leave Japan and go to live in Canada, where I had a job with the federal government, as a research technician with the Arctic Biological Station, studying the great whales.

Unlike most foreigners who came to Japan expressly to study martial arts, I never had any intention of returning and becoming a professional teacher. For me, Karate was a personal battle with my egocentricities, and I did not want to make a career out of that fight. I had another path to follow, and in this path Karate would help me, steady me.

My mother-in-law had bought me Japanese formal dress, and with great patience and peals of laughter from my wife, she had taught me how to wear it properly, and how to tie the complicated folded bow that brought the long tapes of the skirt-like "hakama" together. Resplendent in this dress, feeling very dignified, I went out to visit my friend Ikeda, and walked along the little lanes, enjoying the crisp coldness of the winter air, the chattering of jays, wind tugging at a scarecrow in a field, high lenticular clouds swimming like fish over the Kanto plain.

At my friend's house, his wife served green tea and sweet cakes, and we shared a small flagon of sake. He too was in formal dress, and we posed together for a photograph in front of the ancient farmhouse. As we went back into the house he noticed that mud was spattered up the back of my hakama.

"See what you have done! This is because you are not walking from the hips, like this!" He demonstrated the gliding walk that is so different from the bobbing swagger of the Westerner. As I walked, the heels of my "zori" had flipped mud up my back. Damn it, I couldn't even walk right! I would have to practice. Under Ikeda's tuition I began to learn how the samurai walked, balance always under fine control, gliding from the hips. He showed me the special geta he used to wear; they had a high, single piece of wood on the sole instead of two pieces, so that the wearer had to balance carefully all the time. These, he said, greatly improved balance and strengthened the hips.

When I got home my mother-in-law cleaned the mud off my new hakama.

Our neighbors were making "mochi," the chewy rice cake which is a favorite New Year dish in Japan. Father and son swung the heavy wooden mallets in an easy rhythm, while the mother, with deft fingers, turned the rice which was placed in a "dish" hollowed out of the top of a hefty zelkova log. They laughed and joked and sang snatches of song while the mallets rose and fell, pounding the rice, slowly changing it into a sticky, gluey mass which could be formed and dried out into cakes. They invited me to try, and after a few swings

I found the rhythm, swung the big mallet, thought of the new moon, and of the two rabbits which Japanese children see in the face of the moon, two rabbits making rice cakes.

Life in Japan, life in Akitsu had grown so familiar to me. Farmers and their wives called out greetings to me, and I knew the names of all their crops, and when they would be harvested. I knew where the crows liked to perch, where the jays nested, where the sparrows ducked in under the eaves. I knew where the old Buddhist statues snuggled away in bushes or bamboo groves by the crossroads, knew the shortest way to the station, knew where the boys went down by the temple to catch loach and tadpoles. Time galloped on. So little time left.

Behind our house, my makiwara was weathered now, and the straw pads had been replaced several times. How many hundreds of hours? Certainly my hands had weapon-nature now, and certainly I used the makiwara as much as ever, yet, strangely, the ugly calluses were beginning to disappear. Perhaps I had learned to strike the board correctly, without losing energy in friction between the straw pad and my skin. I believed that the continual pounding and tempering of my limbs had passed the stages of pain and tissue damage, and had begun to be a tempering of mind-forces. I drew comparisons with the pounding of the rice cakes and the personal battle with the makiwara. Force of blows changed the nature of both substances that were capable of change. Rice cakes would be made, hands forged.

When using the makiwara I had no good concept of the passing of time. Ten minutes, or one hour, the difference would have to be measured in the number of blows struck, or in the number of drops of sweat that dripped off my nose or ran down my chest. There seemed to be no difference in level of fatigue or in time. To avoid annoying my family, who perhaps awaited me for dinner, I would have to face the makiwara with the number of blows to be executed already decided against the time available to me. The easy, rhythmic working of my body, the endless variations of techniques that could be practiced were of great joy to me. But the makiwara's nature as a target had changed. It was no longer an obstacle. In attacking it, its hardness or its resistance were no longer noticeable. It merely occupied a space in which I sought to place my technique. I struck through it, and not at it.

The iron geta were kept under the porch step. Red paint had worn off their sides, and where the heels and balls of my feet met the metal it was polished and silvery. The sides had become rusty and indented from hard stones on the road. They had lost the alien quality of newness.

My friends, especially Ikeda, had taught me new things about perception; that great familiarity with a thing can also open and widen the window of the mind to new things about the old. The most treasured bowls used by the tea masters were old ones, ones that bore, in their perfection, imperfections. The old and the new were separated by illusion. Constant use could veil the eyes, yet with increased perception the illusion could be torn, as we tore aside the window we made in our hands at the beginning of the "Kanku Dai" kata, widen vision so that old things could take on newer, deeper colors, finer textures.

Ah, time in Japan was so short. The Eve of the New Year came, and in my formal Japanese dress, with my wife, I went out close to midnight and walked to the temple. Here, as it was all over Japan, the great bell

welcomed in the New Year. There were several people at the temple, but it wasn't crowded, so that those there felt a party spirit, and exchanged pleasantries with others. The priest's wife served all visitors with bowls of sweet sake soup, made from the curds of sake, hot, nutritious, and traditional fare for this season. Young men vied with each other for the honor of sounding the great bell. They seized the heavy ropes, started to swing the huge log, a few inches at first, then more and more until the log drove at the side of the bell like a whale ramming a ship. Deep, long, soft and loud, happy and sad, the vibrations of the bell filled all spaces and caused solid things to tremble. It would be sounded one hundred and eight times.

"Why don't you try?" invited the priest. Urged by the others, I climbed the platform and grabbed the rope. Through it I could feel a slight tremor in the log above my head, hanging down under the little roof. Wind in the trees. Starlight on the curved eaves of the temple roof. Light from the windows of the house behind. Flickering shadows from inside the wide open doors of the temple itself. The bell before me, huge, dark and solemn, humming very softly to itself still. Gradually I magnified the swing of the log until it had far more strength than I, wider, wider until it reared back and rammed the bell so that the sound hurtled us all into the New Year.